The Ford Mustang
1964–1973

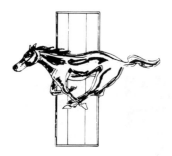

Acknowledgements

Special thanks to the following groups and individuals who lent their time and work to help compile this book:

Ford Motor Company, from which most of the pictures and information in this book is derived.

Paul McLaughlin of the Mustang Owner's Club in Albuquerque, New Mexico, who drew the sketches.

Gerald Wagner of the Shelby Owners of America, Wichita, Kansas.

Motorbooks International, publisher of *The Production Figure Book for U.S. Cars,* from which the production figures in this book are derived.

Jay Holmes of the Street and Strip Speed Shop in Pampa, Texas.

Harold Barrett Ford of Pampa, Texas.

Carl Clark, Vicki Gilbert, Jay Ketelle, and Monte Pearson.

The Ford Mustang

–1964–1973

by Jerry Heasley

TAB BOOKS

BLUE RIDGE SUMMIT, PA. 17214

FIRST EDITION

FIRST PRINTING—FEBRUARY 1979
SECOND PRINTING—FEBRUARY 1980

Copyright © 1979 by TAB BOOKS

Printed in the United States of America

Library of Congress Cataloging in Publication Data

Heasley, Jerry, 1949-
    The Ford Mustang—1964-1973.

    Includes index.
    1. Mustang automobile. I. Title.
TL215.M8H4   629.22′22   78-11175
ISBN 0-8306-9856-6
ISBN 0-8306-2048-6 pbk.

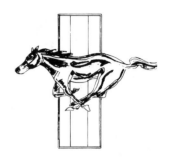

About the Author

Jerry Heasley is a writer and inventor with an abiding interest in old cars. He has owned a variety of them, but post-war special interest Fords are his favorites. As to Mustangs—well, he has owned "about a dozen of them, most 1965 and 1966 models." That seems fair for a Mustang author. "Oh," Heasley recalls, "I've also owned a few late model Mustang convertibles...."

Heasley is 29 years old, was born in Oklahoma and raised there, lived for a year on a farm in Pennsylvania, and since then has lived on the plains of West Texas. He is a graduate of West Texas State University with a major in math and plenty of work in physics.

Heasley is a frequent contributor to *Old Cars* newspaper, the bible of the car collecting hobby/business. He has compiled many prices for the *Old Cars Price Guide,* the most honored and respected such source.

Heasley is probably best known for the heartfelt thanks and tears of gratitude produced by his book, *The Production Figure Book for U.S. Cars.* Unbelievably, there were no accessible figures for a great many makes of American cars. Editors, authors, researchers, dealers and owners were extremely frustrated in the booming and volatile hobby of car collecting. Then Heasley went to work and two years later emerged from his mountain of research with the famed

Jerry Heasley

book that authoritatively answered the question, "How many were made?"

Now, again, he has responded to a tremendous need with this book, *Mustang–1964-1973*. Even so well known a car and one so recently produced has lacked a forthright, detailed, analytical and accurate description for every model of every year for the famed First Generation.

Contents

Introduction.. 11

1 **1964/65: Spectacular First Years**.. 27
The Debut-Planned for Success—Remarkable Public Reaction
Everywhere—1964, 1964½, 1965 are the Same Model—Options
for Complete Change—Standard Six—First of Six—The Short-
Lived 260 V-8—A Trio of 289 V-8s—The Four-Speeds and the
Cruise-O-Matic—Desirability, Distinctions and Accents—Interior
Variations for Multiple Characters—And Still More Options—
Heavy-Duty Units Helped Suspension—Dimensions and
Capacities—Enter Shelby and the GT-350.

2 **1966: Record Sales, No Competition**....................................47
Just Meet the Demand!—607,000 Built in Eight Bodies—Option
List Passes 100—Four Engines Include One Six—The Hotter V-8s
as Before—Minor Changes Distinguish Model Year—Lots of New
'66 Options—Standard Panel Better, Better Seats Optional—
Suspension the Same: Needs Help—Shelby GT-350 Again and
the Rent-a-Racer.

3 **1967: New Styling and Rivals Arrive**.................................... 61
New Body Styles Lead Lineup—Arrival of the Big Block 390—
Many Virtues of the 390—Select Shift Simulates Manual Shift—
Many 1967 Styling Changes—Options Deluge Continues—
Dimensions Up All Around—Many Variations of New Panel—
Interior Options in Profusion—All Chassis Mounts Rubber-
Bushed—Significant Brake Improvements—HD and Competition
Suspension Packs—Shelby GT-500 Joins GT-350.

4 **1968: First Among Muscle Cars** 77
Bodies Similar But Big New Engines—Many Former Extras Now
Standard—Most Power Train Choices So Far—New 302 V-8
Joins the Lineup—427 and 428 Big Blocks Wedged In—Styling
Changes Distinguish Model—Decor, Paint and Protection
Options—Interior Choices up to Luxury Level—A Little More Sus-
pension Attention—Peak Year for Shelbys.

5 **1969: Major Changes and Ten Engines** 93
Mach I Led Fastback Boom—Standard Features Rundown—
Convertible & Fastback, Standards & Options—Boss 302 & 429,
Road Racing & Drags—Ten Engines Including Two Sixes—The
Wildest Boss Yet—New 352 Windsor Was Favorite—428 Cobra
Jet & Super Cobra Jet—Sudden Growth, Length & Weight—Sheet
Metal Changes—Rear Styling and Spoilers—Interior, Fancy and
Comfortable—Changes in Suspension and Shelbys.

6 **1970: Still No. 1 But Fading** 111
Rundown of the Standard Hardtop—Grande and Convertible
Features—Boss 302 and Boss 429 Continued—Two Sixes and
Five V-8s—Four-Speed with Two Ratios—Differing Windsor and
Cleveland 351s—Last Time for the Cobra Jets—Slight Styling
Changes—High-Back Seats Lead Interior Features—Flair Group
of Options New—Important Suspension Improvements—
Dimensions of the 70's and the Last of the Shelbys.

7 **1971: Longer, Lower, Wider** 127
Production and Body Lineup—Grande, Convertible and
Sportsroof Features—Boss 351 in the Sportsroof—Last Produc-
tion Super Car—V-8's Include Low and High Output 351's—Last
Year for the 429 Cobra Jet—Complete Change in Appearance—
Sides and Rooflines All Different—Much Simplified Convertible
Top—New Look at the Rear—Still Fancier Interiors—All-New
Panel for 1971—Wider Car, Better Handling—Important Steering
Changes—Wider, Longer and Lower.

8 1972: Start of the Last Roundup 143
Sales Down but Still Leading—Engines on Regular, Six Models—Luxury Grande, Disappearing Convertible—Just Four Engines & Strange HPs—Performance 351 & High Performance Version—Very Few Outside Changes—Inside Changes & Buzzer Reminders—Convertible Interior Upgraded—Suspensions and Dimensions Stay the Same.

9 1973: The Last of the First 153
Last Convertible in 5-Body Lineup—Grande, Sportsroof, and Mach I Features—Doubled Sales for Last Convertible—One Performance Engine Remains—Urethane Bumper on All Models—Full and ¾ Vinyl Roofs in Six Colors—Continued Luxury Interiors—Handling Adapted to Radials.

10 1964 – 1973: Mustang Value Guide.................................. 163
Other Factors Affect Price—Vehicle Classes.

Appendices

    All Mustang Engines... 169

    All Mustang Transmissions 171

    All Mustang Rear Axles..................................... 173

Index... 175

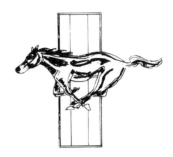

Introduction

Although the immediate development program of the Mustang began in the early Sixties, the first generation cars built from 1964 through 1973 have roots as deep as the company Henry Ford started in the early part of this century. The collector interest in these "early" Mustangs derives from their particular merits and immense popularity when new, and also from the rich heritage of the Ford Motor Company.

The Mustangs of 1964-1973 share the goals and end results of other famous Fords, most notably the Model T (1908-1927), the Model A (1927-1931), and the early V-8's (1932-1953). The Mustangs comprise a fourth major group of collector Fords with the same characteristics as the earlier cars—mass production, great popularity, affordable price, performance image, trend-setting contributions.

LINKS TO THE MODEL T AND MODEL A

For example, the Model T enabled millions of Americans to own their first automobiles because of its affordable price. At one point in 1925, the "tin lizzie" sold for as low as $260 in roadster form. In 1964, the Mustang sold for a relatively low $2,368 for the two-door hardtop, and in less than a year and a half, over a million Americans were driving their first "sports car." If the well-heeled performance buff severely objected to calling the little "ponycar" of the mid Sixties a sports car, he should have heard the gripes of Model T competitors who actually complained that the "T" was not really a true car, but nothing more than mere transportation. The Mustang satisfied the appetite of the man who wanted a sports car, and the Model T satisfied the demand of those who wanted a basic automobile.

Another of the most collected and desired cars of the twentieth century is the Ford Model A, built from 1927 to 1931. After its introduction, admirers called it the "baby Lincoln" because it shared the simple and pleasing lines of Ford Motor Company's expensive, classic Lincoln Model L's of the late Twenties. The Mustang, introduced in 1964, reminded Ford buyers of a "baby Thunderbird" because it shared the flashiness and luxury options of Ford Division's high-priced, very popular full-sized "T-Birds" of the Sixties.

Other similarities abound linking the Model A with the Mustang. During the development period of the "A"—the six-month shutdown of the Ford factory between May 31,1927 and December 2, 1927—the American public eagerly awaited a new breed of car with the impact of the former Model T. During the development of the Mustang—about a three-year lead time prior to 1964— Americans came to associate the name Mustang with engineering advances and looked for a new, exciting car to emerge from Dearborn; perhaps with the good looks of the two-seater Thunderbirds of 1955-56-57.

When the Model A debuted, it let loose excitement second to Charles Lindberg's incredible non-stop flight from New York to Paris that year. The Mustang's introduction day, heavily aided by television, radio, newspaper, and magazine advertising, rated about a second in excitement to a 1964 Beatles' concert as dealer showrooms across the country filled with people. Another curious analog, although unrelated to the cars, is the fact that during the summer of 1927 while the Model A was under development, Babe Ruth hit his record-breaking 60 home runs. That record stood until Roger Maris of the same New York Yankees hit a record-breaking 61 home runs in the summer of 1961, the time when the Mustang was under development.

From botton to top—Mustang I, Mustang II, a 1965 Mustang two-door hardtop, and the extremely rare 1965 Mustang GT-350.

BENEFITS OF FORD'S PERFORMANCE IMAGE

The mention of the mass-produced Ford V-8's of the Thirties, Forties, and early Fifties brings to mind a history of "hot rod" Fords. For the most part of a half-century, the youth of America chose the Model T, the Model A, and finally the more expensive flathead V-8 to "hop up" with aftermarket speed accessories. Although it took several years after the introduction of the V-8 for the mass of performance seekers to give up their rodded four-cylinder T's and A's, the added cylinders and design of the V-8 really got America into the performance scene. Especially after the end of World War II in

13

1945, and until the introduction of the overhead valve V-8 in the mid Fifties, the flathead was the favorite of the youth. The early 30's Fords (now affordable to the youth market and with enough V-8 aftermarket speed accessories readily available), were the ones to build into "sports cars."

The Ford Mustang hit the scene at the right time to be a part of Ford's renewed interest in racing in the early Sixties. The first cars got to use the newly developed small block 260 and larger bore 289, the latter available in a high-performance 271 horsepower version. But these are humble beginnings compared to the impressive list of factory-engineered performance engines added during the life span of the car. Mustangs offered factory-built super cars that could blow the doors off most anything on the street.

IACOCCA'S HUNCH AND PROJECT T-5

Until the fall of 1963, Mustang was known as Project T-5, and referred to within the company as the Turino. Project T-5 started as an idea in the brain of Lee Iacocca, the young, 36-year-old, general manager of Ford Division who replaced the older Robert S. McNamara in November, 1960. Iacocca believed that a market existed for a new breed of car, a young person's car, perhaps, with a sporty look and appeal in an inexpensive package. He wanted a car priced under the $2,500 level, a sort of a poor man's Thunderbird; and, although not a car to compete in the more expensive domestic and foreign sports car market, one that would satisfy the longing of that mass of people that wanted to drive a sports car.

Ford roughly defined this car's competition as the bucket-seated Corvair Monza, which in the early Sixties racked up impressive sales of about a quarter of a million per year for Chevrolet. Still, Project T-5 envisioned a new breed of automobile with no directly competitive counterpart. With these loosely defined goals, a market research group set out to confirm or deny, seek out and define what market, if any, existed corresponding to the hunch of Iacocca.

Market research, with a large staff of 20 persons, uncovered several significant facts. Of major importance was the realization that members of the post World War II baby boom were entering the car buying age. Researchers computed that during the 1960's, the 15-29 age group would increase by a startling 40% to a total of 50.5

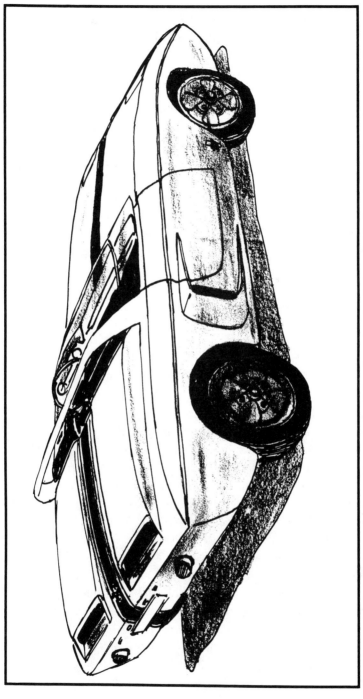

The Mustang I carried the Mustang name and boasted a host of exotic engineering features, but had no chance of becoming a production car.

million! Iacocca called these young people the "buyingest age group in history," and was probably the first auto executive in Detroit to capitalize on this knowledge.

Ford researchers further analyzed that the 18-34 age group would account for about one-half of the increase in new car sales during the Sixties. Also, the number of families earning over $10,000 per year was increasing and expected to expand by 156% between 1960 and 1975. These families would likely buy second and third cars that would suit the tastes and desires of the younger, new drivers. These younger drivers wanted features like bucket seats, floor-shifts, two-door models rather than four-door models, room for four people rather than room for only two people, sporty and stylish looks in a smaller car with performance, and an inexpensive price tag. Ford researchers confirmed the market envisioned by Iacocca; and Iacocca felt that a new type of car appealing as planned to the growing youth population would also draw the broadest mass interest of the general populace.

1962 MUSTANG I—AN EFFECTIVE TEASER

In these pre-production years (1961-1964), with somewhere around 20 clay model designs proposed for the new car, and concurrent market research that was one of the largest in automobile history, two show cars, Mustang I and Mustang II, now stand out as logical steps one and two respectively on the way to the April, 1964, production car. Troutman-Barnes of Los Angeles, California, built the Mustang I although the advance styling studios of Ford Motor Company designed the little two-seater in January, 1961.

When shown to the public at the Watkins Glen Grand Prix in the fall of 1962, Mustang I was a rocket-shaped, low-slung, two-passenger aluminum-bodied roadster of a slight 1500 pounds with bucket seats, tubular frame, four-wheel independent suspension, and a 160 horsepower Taunus-Cardinal V-4 engine mounted "amidship"—between the driver and the rear wheels—with a trans-axle unit. The driver's seat was not adjustable, but the accelerator, brake, and clutch could be adjusted fore and aft for a total travel of four inches. It had a permanently fixed roll bar integral with the frame and a host of other exotic engineering features such as the

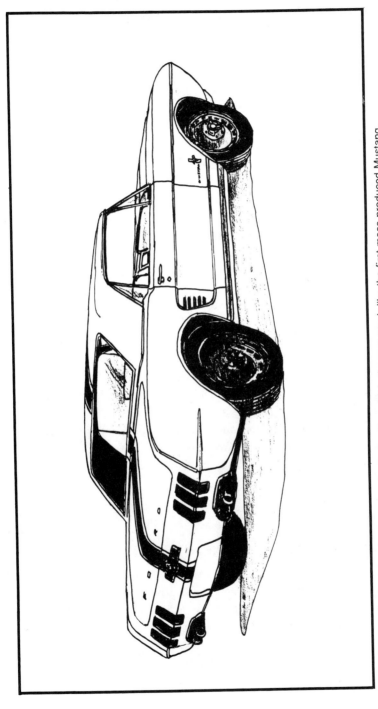

The Mustang II is the design that Ford "productionized", and it looks very much like the first mass-produced Mustang.

twin rear-mounted radiators cooled by natural air flow or electric fans.

Of course the Mustang I did not have a chance of becoming a production car and was more of an engineering show for publicity; but it carried the Mustang name and was a part of the new youthful image of Ford Motor Company.

MUSTANG II—THE SERIOUS PROTOTYPE

The Mustang II however, designed in August of 1962, was the prototype of the first Mustang or the design that was "productionized." Its requirements included a price less than or equal to $2,500, a weight of 2500 pounds, a length of no more than 180 inches overall, plus a floorshift, a snappy six-cylinder engine, bucket seats in the front and a bench seat in the back, a lengthy list of optional equipment, and a sporty design with the long hood and short deck look then best described by Ford as "demure enough for church-going, racy enough for the drag strip, modish enough for the country club."

Ford planned to use Ford Falcon and Fairlane light-car suspension components, engines, and driveline early in the planning of the new car. The main job of engineering consisted of keeping the Mustang II's style and clean lines intact while giving the car structural integrity. Ford did use a new frame although they did not develop it specifically for the Mustang. Called a platform-type frame, it consisted of sturdy siderails with five welded crossmembers that form a base. Because its construction was the result of previous engineering at Ford Motor Company, its use did not add expense to the introduction of the all-new car and also helped product planners beat the price goal of $2,500.

FIRST, THE MUSTANG WAS A COUGAR

By December of 1962, engineering had structured the car into the form of the first Mustang, and it looked much like the Mustang II prototype. Because Cougar was its working title, however, the grille of the productionized Mustang II contains a cougar emblem in the center of the grille; the car had not yet been named. With the addition of bumpers, the grille mouth was raised a bit, and the sheet metal below the bumpers was not tucked as far under the car on the

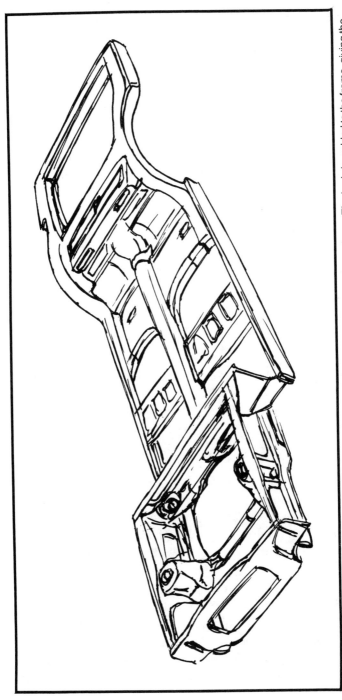

Ford's platform-type frame consists of sturdy siderails with five welded crossmembers that form a base. The body is welded to the frame, giving the Mustang a "uni-body" construction. This body frame unit is lightweight, strong, and contributes to a quiet ride.

"Cougar." Also, the production car did not have the metal bars in front of the headlight beams, and the profile of the front fenders did not have the pronounced vee shape.

In the year and four months remaining until introduction day, Ford named the car, instigated a retooling program of $50,000,000, and heavily promoted the new car in what became a record-breaking year for the United States automobile industry in sales.

With respect to naming the new car, Iacocca favored Mustang over two other likely choices, Turino and Cougar. Turino was a logical choice because the grille of the car was designed with an open mouth like the racing cars Iacocca saw at Turino, Italy. Ford Studios, who designed the car, used the name Cougar as a working title. But the favored name of Mustang, also used during Project T-5, probably symbolized and aligned the public with the youthful themes Iacocca tried to build from the beginning of the project—youth, speed, freedom, etc.

The name Mustang gives its owner an image extension; its connotation brings visions of a cowboy astride a spirited horse riding across the plains of the great west. The nickname of the Mustang, "ponycar," also lent itself to a general term for a new breed of car produced in Detroit. Its earliest competitor, the Plymouth Barracuda, was joined by later competitors like the Chevrolet Camaro, the Pontiac Firebird, the Mercury Cougar, and the American Motors Javelin.

THIS BOOK: BY MODEL YEAR IN DETAIL

The purpose of this book is to look at the first generation Mustangs with respect to the model year lineup, the standard features, the engines and accompanying powertrain, distinguishing exterior and interior design features, options and accessories, etc., to enable one to differentiate the various Mustangs in relation to one another.

First, the cars are separated by chapters on a model year basis. Each chapter contains a breakdown of cars into body numbers, and a listing of standard equipment making up each of the body styles. A general treatment of production figures is also given which, like the chapters, is on a model year basis. The listing of standard equipment is derived from the original factory sales brochures and is very useful in describing the cars for each year.

Ford had not yet chosen a name for the car as late as 1963. Because Cougar was its working title, however, the grille of the productionized car contained a Cougar emblem.

From this point, the book differentiates the engines powering the various cars with a more general treatment of transmission and rear axle combinations (because of their susceptibility to change and availability with the progression of the model year). Beginning with the introduction of the Mustang in 1964, the number of engines built to a maximum in 1969 and then dissipated to a minimum in 1973.

Mustangs benefited from the factory-sponsored racing program of the Sixties and the rise of the high performance, factory-prepared engines. During this time, "hot rodding" moved from the backyards of America to the automobile factories, and performance buffs could buy their hot rods ready to go from the showroom floor of their local dealerships.

POWER YEARS WITH "BOSS" AND "WEDGE"

In 1967, Ford fitted the big block 390 CID engine into the Mustang; in 1968 they added the 427 "wedge," and at mid-year the 428 Cobra Jet. But the best was yet to come, and 1969 sports car fans saw the "Boss" 302, the 428 Super Cobra Jet, and the awesome "Boss" 429 installed in the lightweight Mustangs.

The high compression, high-performance engines began to drop from the lineup around the 1970 model year, and especially the latter part of 1971. However, the full Mustang lineup with its revised front-end geometry got to use the big 429 Cobra Jets for a full year in 1971.

Then, just when the full-performance scene was ready for a quantum leap forward, Ford dropped out of racing and quit promoting the high-performance cars. By 1972 and 1973, Mustangs carried the former super car looks without the ultra-high performance.

Federal emission controls, sky-rocketing insurance rates, and decreasing sales are three reasons for the end of the evolution of the factory-built high-compression, high-output engine. Cars built prior to 1968 are unregulated on a federal basis with respect to control of exhaust emissions, of which the main three are hydrocarbons (HC), carbon monoxide (CO), and nitrous oxide (NO). But the 1968 and later cars are regulated, and federal standards became more rigid with the passing of every two years. The regulation of the oxides of nitrogen and the switch to low lead fuels in the early Seventies put an end to the high compression engines.

Another pre-production car, but with the Mustang identification. Note the absence of the large metal spears flanking the Mustang emblem in the grille.

STYLING DESCRIBED BY YEAR GROUPS

After looking at the body styles and applicable engines, interior and exterior styling changes are described from one year to the next. Since Ford restyled the Mustang in 1967, 1969, and 1971, the cars in the groups 1964-1966, 1967-1968, 1969-1970, and 1971-1973 look about alike. After a description of the 1964/65 model, the 1966 cars are described with respect to changes and refinements.

As a group, these first Mustangs are perhaps the most sought after and collected, although they achieved the highest production. The major restyling in 1967 produced a slightly longer and wider car with a revised front-end geometry. The 1967 and 1968 cars, however, are very similar to the original; many of the options and accessories of the 1965 and 1966 cars are applicable to the 1967 and 1968 cars.

Some people feel that the character of the Mustang changed in 1969; Ford's major restyling produced a larger car with the looks of a supercar and a plush interior. The lineup also expanded for the first time, as Ford added the Mach I sportsroof and the Grande hardtop, plus the "Boss" 302 and "Boss" 429 as submodels of the sportsroof body style.

The radical restyling of the Mustang in 1971 produced the 1971 through 1973 cars, sometimes called the "born of the track" Mustangs. Wheelbase increased for the first time in 1971, a mere one inch; but these cars look much larger than any of their predecessors.

OPTIONS/ACCESSORIES DISTINGUISHED/DESCRIBED

Options and accessories are factory and/or dealer installed, and number well over 100 for some years. An option is an item that replaces part of the standard equipment. An accessory, however, is an extra-cost piece of equipment that is added to a car to improve its beauty or usefulness.

Major options and accessories are listed with their basic application and makeup. For example, the GT Equipment Group of 1966 applied to models first having the 225 or 271 horsepower 289 V-8 engines.

Of course, every option and accessory is not listed, as Ford added many during the middle of the model year, some of which later dropped from availability with little mention in catalogs, literature, etc. The 1964-1968 cars especially offered a large number of options and accessories. Ford could have made every Mustang unique with the different combinations of accessories alone. A trend developed in 1969 in which Ford fitted cars with a combination of options and accessories that gave the car its own distinctive name and model number, as in the case of the Grande hardtop or the Mach I sportsroof.

PERFORMANCE DEMANDS EVOLVED SUSPENSIONS

Suspension systems on the 1964-1973 Mustangs are of the independent coil type in the front and the leaf spring type in the rear. The coil springs in the front rest on top of the upper arm supports and extend up towers in the sheet metal of the body to either side of the engine. The front shock absorbers are mounted within the coil springs. Ford sold optional heavy duty or competition suspension systems throughout the life of the Mustang.

In the early years, the basic configuration did not change; a special handling package, for example, included stiffer rate springs, heavy-duty shock absorbers, and an increased diameter front stabilizer bar. With each succeeding year, however, the handling characteristics improved. The 1967's, for example, use a slightly re-engineered front-end geometry with lower upper arm pivots.

As the Mustang placed cars in the muscle-car field, the need for improved suspension grew. For example, in the latter part of 1969 Ford started staggering the rear shocks on certain high-performance cars for increased rear-end stability.

Steering and brake systems also use basic systems that remained about the same throughout the life of the first generation cars. The steering gear of Mustangs is of the recirculating-ball type with a certain steering gear ratio—for example, 27:1 ratio on cars with power steering. In 1971, Ford offered a variable rate steering gear with cars using the competition suspension. The hydraulic brake systems of the Mustangs also remained about the same throughout 1964-1973. But the 1967 models, for example, begin using the dual hydraulic master cylinder for added safety.

SHELBY MUSTANG COVERAGE, 1966-1970

The end of each chapter for the model years 1966 through 1970 contains a brief description of the Shelby Mustangs. And the 1965 model year contains a complete list of standard equipment to reveal the performance determination of the first Shelbys. With each succeeding year, these custom cars substituted more luxury in place of the all-out sports car features.

In addition to a look at the makeup of the Mustangs, the start of each chapter indicates the popularity of the cars when new by looking at some of the facts of the particular model year. The highly desirable collector cars or special interest old cars are usually the ones which the new car buyer also highly prized. For as the first glimpse of a sparkling new Mustang in 1965 quickened the heart beat of the car fan, the re-discovery of that same car in a later year produces a similar fever.

Jerry Heasley

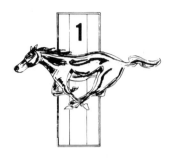

1964/65:
Spectacular First Years

The soon-to-open New York World's Fair, wrote one writer, was "the most popular attraction of the century"; the first unmanned Gemini spacecraft blasted off from Cape Kennedy on a successful mission orbiting the earth; President Lyndon B. Johnson battled for postponement of a possible crippling nationwide rail strike while the 1964 baseball season opened boasting such all-time greats as Mickey Mantle, Roger Maris, Willie Mays, Sandy Koufax, and Roberto Clemente.

Amid these current events, the covers of *Time* and *Newsweek* pictured the arrival of a new model car from Detroit. Presidential hopefuls like George Wallace, Hubert Humphrey, and Barry Goldwater entered primaries in this election year. But periodicals such as *Life, Esquire, U.S. News and World Report,* and *Business Week* also focused attention on the arrival of this new car.

THE DEBUT—PLANNED FOR SUCCESS

The coming of the Ford Mustang in the spring of 1964 carried that weight. *Life* magazine called it a "sports car for the masses," *Newsweek's* cover read "The Mustang—Newest Breed Out of Detroit," while *Time* called the Mustang a sports car and "one of the most heralded and attention-getting cars in autodom's history." Although largely contrived, the introduction of the Mustang is surrounded by indications of an immense success. On April 13, 1964, just four days prior to introduction day, 124 members of the press were invited to a special preview showing of the Mustang at the Ford Pavillion at the New York World's Fair. After the showing, reporters were paired in Mustangs for a 750-mile road rally to Detroit. The experience of the trip paid off for Ford the next week in favorable reports written by the journalists.

Official introduction, April 17, 1964, was preceded the previous evening by simultaneous advertising in prime time on NBC, CBS, and ABC national television networks, with an estimated audience of 29 million. Ford tried to reach the most people in the shortest amount of time. One hundred Holiday Inns displayed new Mustangs, air travelers ran into Mustangs at 15 major air terminals throughout the country, four top television shows gave away Mustangs as prizes, and billboards displayed ads for the car in 170 locations with the suggested retail price prominently visible. About 2600 newspapers contained announcement ads delivered to over 2200 markets across the United States, contributing to the surge of visitors that came to the showrooms to see the car—and buy it.

REMARKABLE PUBLIC REACTION EVERYWHERE

A college study resource paper published by the Educational Affairs Department of Ford Motor Company in 1974 listed the following results of Mustang's simple and forceful ad campaign that ominously used the theme "the unexpected." In San Francisco, a truck driver, "apparently thrown into a trance by the sight of the car, ... could not take his eyes away, and drove his truck straight through the showroom window." In Chicago, a Ford dealer felt obliged "to lock the doors of the Mustangs in his showroom because so many people were trying to crowd into the cars at once, they were in danger of injuring themselves." In Pittsburgh, a dealer could not get a Mustang off the wash rack, "because of the crowd of people pressing below." Even more unbelievable, (or unexpected?) is the story about the dealership where 15 customers wanted the same Mustang. The successful buyer is reported to have slept the night in his new car so that "they would not sell it out from under me before my check clears in the morning."

One of the first model Mustangs. Note the optional backup lights, rocker panel molding below the door, and the spinner-type full wheel covers. Although the rocker panel molding came as part of an optional accent group, one could order it separately, as on this convertible.

Dealers couldn't get enough Mustangs to meet the demand, and by the end of four months, 100,000 traveled the streets. Soon, Mustangs rolled from assembly lines at the rate of 7,000 per week and climbed among the five top-selling car models in America.

However, the first quarter automobile sales of 1964, the immediate three months before Mustang reached the market, set a record as the highest in history to that date—largely the result of a growing population coupled with the increase of the multi-car family during prosperous years. Also contributing to the success of the Mustang was the fact that as a "new breed of car," a specialty car, it had no direct competition. Apparently, the Mustang sported the look that the public wanted with its long hood and short deck, a look that would soon be imitated. For now the Corvair by Chevrolet and the Barracuda by Plymouth most closely compared with Ford's Mustang. But the Corvair was rear-engined and not able to handle a larger motor while the Barracuda shared body lines with the utilitarian Plymouth Valiant. Mustang claimed its own unique body highly distinguishable in a parking lot and gave its owner optional V-8 power.

1964, 1964½, 1965 ARE THE SAME MODEL

From introduction day on April 17, 1964 until the official opening of the 1965 model year that fall, Mustang offered two body styles—the two-door hardtop and the convertible. The line-up added the fastback body style for 1965. Some people call the first Mustangs 1964 or 1964½ models rather than 1965's. Cars produced through the end of the 1965 model year, however, are the same model car.

Official Ford Motor Company production figures place the manufacture of 92,705 two-door hardtops, Body #65A, within the 1964 model year along with 28,822 convertibles, Body #76A, for a total run of 121,538. For model year 1965, a total of 559,538. For model year 1965, a total of 559,451 left assembly lines with the demand still growing. The lineup for 1964 and 1965, then, looks as follows:

1964	Body	#65A	Two-Door Hardtop
		#76A	Convertible

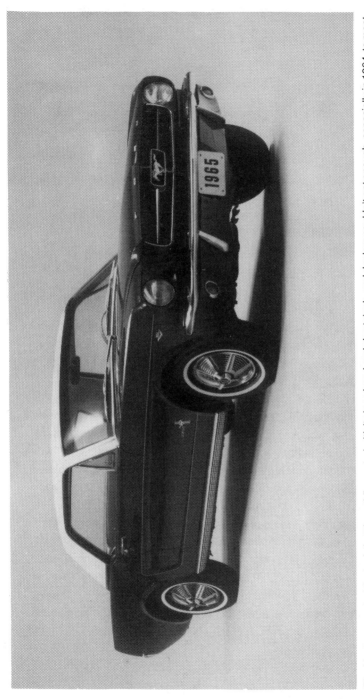

The Mustang sported the look that the public wanted with its long hood and short deck, and dealers couldn't get enough, especially in 1964, to meet the demand. This car carries the optional accent group. Note the "Tiffany" stripe, rocker panel molding, and deleted air scoop treatment.

1965	Body	#63A	Two-Door Fastback—Standard
		#63B	Two-Door Fastback—Luxury
		#65A	Two-Door Hardtop—Standard
		#65B	Two-Door Hardtop—Luxury
		#65C	Two-Door Hardtop—Bench Seats
		#76A	Convertible/Standard
		#76B	Convertible—Luxury
		#76C	Convertible—Bench Seats

The most popular body style for 1965 was the two-door hardtop with 419,260 produced. Fastback production reached 77,079 with just 5,776 of these in luxury trim. Convertible production totaled 73,112.

OPTIONS FOR COMPLETE CHANGE

The 1964/65 Mustangs featured standard equipment and specifications that, in this author's opinion, moved it out of a possible compact car category. With the long list of possible optional equipment and accessories, Mustangs could be tailored to build, for example, a sports car, a family car, a luxury car, a status car, an economy car, etc. Mustang first capitalized on this concept on a mass scale, and if not originating the idea, spread it to other car manufacturers in Detroit and the rest of the automobile world.

For $2,368 FOB Detroit, the two-door hardtop included individually adjustable, deep-foam bucket seats, padded instrument panel, full-wheel covers, all-vinyl or cloth-vinyl-trimmed interiors, color-keyed wall-to-wall carpeting, sports steering wheel with bright metal horn arms, cigarette lighter, two automatic courtesy lights, glove box light, floor shift three-speed manual transmission, 170 CID six-cylinder (200 CID starting in 1965), heater/defroster, front seat belts, front arm rests, electric windshield wipers, safety-yoke door latches, curved side glass, wrap-around front bumper, bumper guards front and rear, alternator (early models in '64 used generators), "sta-ful" battery, and Ford's "twice-a-year" maintenance features. The maintenance schedule consisted of 6,000 miles or six months—whichever came first—between oil changes and minor chassis lubrication. Major chassis lubes came every 36,000 miles or three years.

The convertible, with a base price of $2,614, presented the standard features of the hardtop (except for the cloth-trimmed vinyl

Ford added the fastback body style at the official beginning of the 1965 model year. With a base price of $2,533, buyers came out in large numbers to grab these.

interior), plus a five-ply, vinyl-bonded top in black, white, or tan with a zip-out window and a matching stretch taut boot to stow the top.

The fastback, advanced at the official beginning of the 1965 model year, included the standard equipment available in the hardtop at a base price of $2,533 with the added extra features of a tinted glass in the large "skylight" rear window, functional louvers just behind the side windows, and a fold-down rear seat that tripled luggage space.

STANDARD SIX—FIRST OF SIX

For 1964/65, Mustangs are found with six different factory original engines applicable to each body style. The previously mentioned 170 and 200 CID powerplants with single one-barrel carburetors are rated at 101 and 120 horsepower respectively. Both engines are smiliar with the intake manifold cast as an integral part of the cylinder head. Bore and stroke of the 200, however, are slightly larger and the engine uses an impressive seven main bearings compared to the four mounting the crankshaft in the smaller 170.

Matched with the standard three-speed manual or optional three-speed "Cruise-O-Matic" transmission mated to the 3.50 rear axle ratio, either six provides snappy performance; zero to sixty miles per hour times fall in the 13-15 second bracket. A four-speed manual transmission, fully synchronized in all forward gears, is designed especially for the six with a wider ratio than that used for the V-8's. The synchronization allows the transmission to be downshifted while moving for better control of the road under different driving conditions. Six-cylinder cars also use their own differential carrier that is integral with the axle housing.

THE SHORT-LIVED 260 V-8

The 260 CID V-8, called the Challenger V-8, is of the overhead valve design, like all Mustang V-8's. The 260, with single two-barrel carburetor was offered on early 1965 models before being dropped in favor of the newer, more popular 289. The 260 has a 164 horsepower maximum at 4400 rpm and uses regular fuel with its moderately low compression ratio of 8.8:1. With a three-speed manual transmission (synchronized on the V-8), or optional Cruise-O-Matic matched to the 3.00 rear axle ratio, the 260 accelerates from 0-60

With the rear seat of the fastback folded down, the Mustang gave its owner a sportier two-seater look as well as a practical excuse for buying a sports car.

mph in the 12-14 second range. Curiously, a four-speed manual was not available with the 260 Challenger.

A TRIO OF 289 V-8S

Three 289 CID engines completed the engine lineup for 1965— a 2-barrel, a 4-barrel, and a 4-barrel high-performance version. Similar to the 260 with stud-mounted rocker arms (for adjustability), and wedge shaped combustion chambers, the 289 offers a larger bore of 4.00 inches (versus the 3.80) with the same stroke of 2.87 inches. The two-barrel version rates a maximum 200 horse-power at 4400 rpm and uses regular fuel with its 9.3:1 compression of the fuel/air mixture. The four-barrel 289 Challenger Special rates a slightly higher 225 horsepower at 4800 rpm with a 10.5:1 compression ratio that requires premium gasoline.

So far, all engines use self-adjusting valves with hydraulic lifters. The 289 Challenger high-performance V-8, however, uses manually adjustable "solid" valve lifters for more precise valve opening and closing, especially needed for the high rpm operation. Its maximum 271 horsepower is reached at a high-revving 6000 rpm. This engine used a manual choke in favor of the automatic choke, a single four-barrel carburetor, and dual exhausts as standard.

THE FOUR-SPEEDS AND THE CRUISE-O-MATIC

In 1965, the four-speed manual was the one transmission listed available with this engine. Fully synchronized, this four-speed uses a closer gear reduction through the forward speeds than that mated to the other V-8's. Standard rear axle ratios were the low-speed 3.89's with the even lower speed 4.11's optional. Limited slip differentials were an extra cost option, and are very desirable extras for both the performance buff and the driver concerned with driving on snow or ice; it divides torque more equally to both rear wheels.

The floor-mounted shift lever of the Cruise-O-Matic three-speed automatic uses a shift pattern with six positions—Park (P), Reverse (R), Neutral (N), Drive 2 (a white dot), Drive 1 (a green dot), and Low (L). In Drive 2, the car starts from rest in second gear and upshifts to high automatically. This driving position is useful for starts on slippery surfaces like ice or snow. The normal driving position, Drive 1, begins in low gear and then automatically shifts to

The newly-developed 289 CID engine that became virtually synonymous with the name Mustang.

second and high gears. Of course, in low gear the transmission stays in low gear until shifted manually.

DESIRABILITY, DISTINCTIONS AND ACCENTS

The Ford Mustang of 1964/65 is a beautiful automobile and highly sought after by collectors. As it was prized by new car owners in the Sixties, it is prized by old car owners, both for its pleasing looks and its performance possibilities.

The front grilled mouth of the original ponycar extends the width of the hood with seven-inch single headlamps to either side. The chromed Mustang emblem in the center of the grille is accented by four bright metal spears and a "honeycomb" metal background in gun metal gray. Mustangs equipped with the GT option (GT Equipment Group), incorporate fog lights in the grille on either side of the horse. The front bumper is called a wrap-around bumper and is accompanied by bumper guards on all models in front of the lower enamel-coated galvanized panel. This panel also contains a license plate recess and turn signal/parking lights.

Script markings on the car include FORD in bright metal block letters at the front edge of the hood, a Mustang emblem and the word MUSTANG in bright block letters behind the front wheel openings, and on V-8 equipped cars, a small "V" insignia opening wide to include the 260, 289, or 289 high performance designations on the side of the front fenders just ahead of the front wheels.

The windshield is angled at a rakish 52½ degrees and trimmed with chrome. Likewise, the curved side vent, side door, and side quarter windows are banded with chromed metal. Cars without the optional accent group contain a simulated air intake scoop and chrome molding that is located just ahead of the rear wheels on the rear quarter panels. This simulated air scoop is deleted, however, on cars ordered with the accent group which contains what is called a "Tiffany" stripe following the body side sculpturing. (Mustang received the Tiffany and Company "Gold Model Award for Excellence in American Design"—the first time a car was so honored.) The accent group also contains a rocker panel molding, except on the fastback.

In the tradition of many sports cars, the wheel openings are circular to completely expose the wheels. The rear of the Mustang features a bumper curved at the outer edges to meet the contours of the sheet metal. The panel above the rear bumper contains the taillight/turn signals to each side with a unique "tri-port" design that uses a bright metal bezel over a single red lens. The screw-off gas cap is located in the center of this panel with appropriate Mustang identification.

Like the front lower panel, the rear lower panel below the rear bumper mounts rear bumper guards as standard equipment, and back-up lamps as an extra cost accessory. In addition to the 16 "Brilliant Diamond Lustre Enamel Single Tones" available for exterior colors, other factory exterior option/accessories include a power-operated convertible top, tinted glass for all windows, tinted glass for the windshield only, a vinyl roof in black or white for the hardtop, deluxe wheel covers, wire wheel covers, and styled steel wheels.

An almost endless number of dealer-installed accessories were added throughout the life span of the car, items like door-edge guards, a license plate frame, a luggage rack, ski rack, spot-light, tonneau cover, and more.

INTERIOR VARIATIONS FOR MULTIPLE CHARACTERS

The interior of the 1964/65 Mustang is designed to blend with the multiple character of the car; i.e., sports car, family car, economy car, etc. For example, the front seats are buckets, but in the hardtop and convertible, a front bench seat model, Body #65C and #76C respectively, could be ordered. It stands to reason then, that the fastback did not offer a bench seat model because of its all-out sports car style. The back seats of the 65's use the "semi-bucket" construction with an uncushioned hard spot in the middle that could seat a small person on short trips. Cars with luxury-trimmed interiors, i.e., seats with embossed pictures of ponies on the vinyl inserts, deluxe steering wheel, and courtesy/warning lights in the door, gave the car further flexibility with respect to taste.

The dashes of the 1964/65 Mustangs, however, use a disappointing Falcon-like instrument cluster in front of the driver in which the speedometer is enclosed in a horizontal case with red warning lights for the oil pressure and water temperature, in addition to the circular fuel and amperage gauges. Cars with the GT Equipment Group, however, use circular dials for the speedometer, oil pressure, and water temperature.

Other features of the GT cars include dual exhausts with bright extensions through the rear panel, fog lamps, disc brakes, special handling package, GT stripes, GT plaques, and GT fuel filler cap. This option was available with all body styles if the optional 225 or 271 horsepower engine was first ordered.

AND STILL MORE OPTIONS

The visibility group, available on all models, included inside nonglare day-night mirror, remote outside mirror, and two-speed windshield wipers and washers. Other interior option/accessories included an air conditioner (except with the 289 high-performance engine), an emergency flasher that operated all four turn signal lights, a fresh air heater/defroster as a delete option at an appropriate cost reduction, padded sun visors (except on convertibles), a Rally-Pac consisting of a clock and tachometer mounted in a twin pod black housing on the steering column, a console, a transistorized AM push-button radio, front seat belts (another delete option), front seat belts with retractors, and two-speed windshield wipers with washers.

Dealer installed option/accessories included such interesting items as a two-way citizens band radio, compass, door-storage compartment, fire extinguisher, floor mats, glove compartment and console glove box lock, a parking brake warning light, a 12-volt map light, litter basket, an inside non-glare day-nite mirror, a circular outside rearview mirror, remote control outside rearview mirror available with matching right-hand non-remote mirror, rear radio seat speaker in the hardtop, rear seat belts, seat belt retractors, tachometers with 6000, 8000, or 9000 rpm readings, and more.

HEAVY-DUTY UNITS HELPED SUSPENSION

Front suspensions of the '65 Mustangs are of the independent coil spring type while the rear suspension is a simple longitudinal leaf spring set up with diagonally-mounted shock absorbers. Handling characteristics, although not outstanding, are good and greatly improved with the optional special handling package. This option,

The dashes of the 1964/65 Mustangs use a disappointing "Falcon"-like instrument cluster in front of the driver.

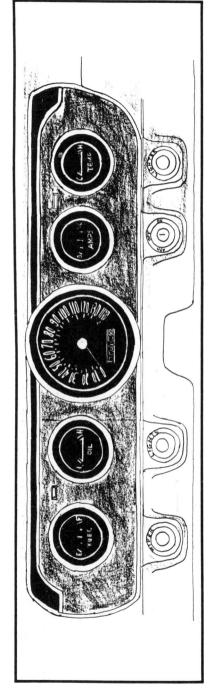

The 1964/65 cars with the GT Equipment Group use circular dials for the speedometer, oil pressure, water temperature, fuel level, and amperage.

standard with the high-performance 289, uses heavier front and rear springs, heavy-duty front and rear shock absorbers, increased diameter front stabilizer bar (from .69 inches with the standard suspension to .84 inches), and a quicker steering ratio of 22:1. The overall steering ratio of the manual system is a contrasting 27:1 with the same turning diameter of 38 feet.

Disc brakes improve the stopping ability of the drum brakes 10-15% on V-8 models and practically eliminate fade during heavy-duty use. However, on the six-cylinder cars, the drums give stopping ability on par with the discs and fade is encountered only after unusually long and hard use. The power brakes, optional in '65, were not available in combination with the discs. The handling package and the front wheel ventilated disc brakes are highly desirable Mustang options and somewhat rare. Drum brakes are self-adjusting, self-energizing with 131 square inches of lining area on six-cylinder cars and 154 square inches on the V-8's. Tires are 6.50 × 13 with four-bolt lug patterns on the sixes with 6.95 × 14's optional. Cars with V-8's use the 6.95 × 14's as standard with a five-bolt lug pattern.

DIMENSIONS AND CAPACITIES

With respect to dimensions and capacities, overall length is 181.6 inches on a 108-inch wheelbase. Width equals 68.2 inches while height of hardtop, convertible, and fastback is 51.5, 51.4, and 51.6 inches, respectively. Eight-cylinder cars have a front track width of 56.0 inches while sixes equal 55.4 inches. Rear track width is the same for sixes and V-8's, 56.0 inches. Representative weights for hardtop, convertible, and fastback are 2562, 2740, and 2621 pounds, respectively, with six-cylinder engines. Usable trunk luggage volume is 9.0 cubic feet for the hardtop, 7.7 for the convertible, and 5.5 for the fastback (18.5 with rear seat folded down). Fuel tank capacity is 16 gallons for all models.

ENTER SHELBY AND THE GT-350

Late in the 1965 model year, the Mustang GT-350 in street and competition versions became available to the public. These cars are extremely rare; 562 of the street version with a $4547 base price

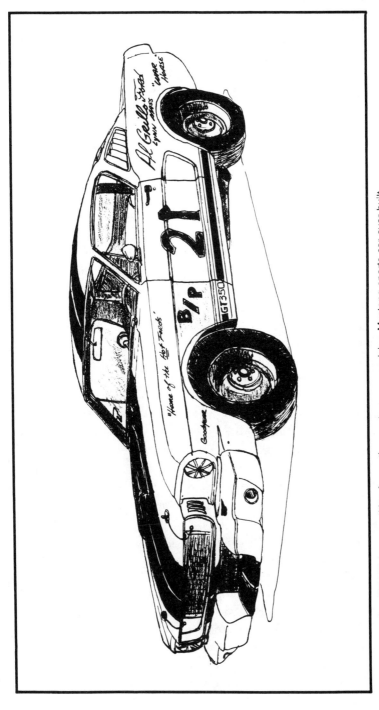

The 1965 Mustang GT-350 in competition form—the most uncompromising Mustang sports car ever built.

were built while a trickling 12 of the competition machines costing $5950 (the "R" models) were built.

Assembled by Carroll Shelby of racing frame in 1965 at Shelby-American, Inc. in Los Angeles, the GT-350 is a fastback stripped and then highly modified to run faster, handle better, and look racier than the regular Mustangs. The competition model could be trailered from the dealership to the drag strip and turn the quarter mile in 14.5 seconds at about 98 mph through the traps—not bad for 1965!

Standard equipment on these Shelbys lists like a 1965 speed shop inventory. The GT-350 street version contained the following standard equipment: Shelby-American prepared 289 CID Cobra V-8 engine rated 306 horsepower at 6000 rpm; special high riser aluminum manifold; center pivot float four-barrel carburetor; specially designed hand-built tubular "tuned" exhaust system featuring straight-through-glass-packed mufflers; finned Cobra aluminum valve covers; extra capacity finned and baffled aluminum oil pan; fully synchronized, Borg-Warner special, Sebring, close-ratio four-speed transmission with lightweight all-alloy case; computer-designed competition suspension geometry; one-inch diameter front anti-roll bar; fully stabilized, torque-controlled rear axle equipped with "No-Spin" limited slip differential; 15-inch diameter wide base steel wheels mounted with 130 mph-rated, Goodyear "High Performance-Blue Dot" tires; Kelsey Hayes front disc brakes with ventilated disc and special full competition pads; wide drum rear brakes with metallic linings; Koni adjustable shock absorbers; trunk-mounted Cobra battery for optimum weight distribution (hood mounted in later cars); lightweight fiberglass hood with integrally-designed functional air scoop; all-black interior with bucket-type seats and Shelby-approved competition "quick release" seat belts; special instrument cluster with tachometer and oil pressure gauge in addition to speedometer, fuel gauge, and water temperature gauge; two-speed electric windshield wipers and washers; woodrim racing steering wheel; 19:1 quick ratio steering; spare wheel cover; heater; and 250 competition side stripe.

The competition version added the following prepared features: fiberglass front lower apron panel; engine oil cooler; large capacity water radiator; front and rear brake cooling assemblies;

34-gallon fuel tank; 3½-inch quick-fill cap; electric fuel pump; large-diameter exhaust pipes; no muffler; five magnesium bolt-on 7 × 15-inch wheels; revised wheel openings; interior safety group—roll bar, shoulder harness, fire extinguisher, flame resistant interior, plastic rear window, aluminum-framed sliding plastic side windows; complete instrumentation—tachometer, speedometer, oil pressure and temperature, water temperature, fuel pressure; full Shelby-American competition prepared and dyno-tuned engine; plus special final track test and adjustments.

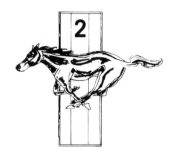

1966:
Record Sales, No Competition

Ford Motor Company sold more cars to date than any model year in history in 1965—2,064,058, and the 1966 model year topped that figure with 2,093,832. Mustang, practically alone in the sporty, specialty car field, contributed to Ford's record sales and helped increase Ford's percentage of the American automobile market at the expense of General Motors, Chrysler, and American Motors.

The 1966 model year begain in the fall of 1965 with Detroit still reeling from the impact of the Mustang but offering no direct competition to challenge the little ponycar. Buick offered the Special and Skylark, Chevrolet sold the Malibu, Oldsmobile built the F-85 Series, Pontiac had the LeMans and GTO, while Plymouth sold the Barracuda for a second year. These cars offered somewhat sporty looks with the basic body lines of their larger sedan models in their respective lineups. Other sketchy competition included the Chevrolet Corvair and the Dodge Charger which did use distinctive, separately styled bodies. But, the Dodge Charger, for example, cost more money with a base price tag of $3122 and lacked versatility with its radical sweptback roof, full width grille with hidden headlights, standard 318 CID V-8 engine, four bucket seats, wheelbase of 118 inches, and overall length of 203 inches. And the Corvair, with its basic looks virtually unchanged from 1965, suffered an incredible 50% drop in sales from the previous model year.

JUST MEET THE DEMAND!

Evidently, Ford did not have a larger incentive for major changes of their beloved Mustang. Ford was more concerned with supplying the demand. While Mustangs galloped from assembly plants at the rate of 13,000 per week, Ford sales brochures urged prospective customers to "Take a Second Look," and "If you thought we couldn't improve on a winner, try Mustang '66!" By the spring of 1966, with more than a million of the ponycars prancing the streets, (enough to make a line of cars bumper to bumper for over 2800 miles!), some automotive analysts wondered whether Mustang would become another phenomenon like the Volkswagen.

By 1966, Mustangs gained a reputation as perhaps the most fault-free Ford ever built. Changes for 1966 included refinements of the grille, the side scoop ornamentation, the wheel covers, and the gas filler cap, plus the addition of a chrome molding around the lip of the hood. The list of options and accessories expanded while padded front arm rests and seat belts front and rear became standard. Ford completely dropped the thirteen-inch wheels in the Mustang line, although the six-cylinder ponies utilized fourteen-inch wheels with the same four-bolt lug pattern seen on the smaller wheels. Cars with V-8's, of course, used the five-bolt lug pattern on fourteen-inch wheels.

607,000 BUILT IN EIGHT BODIES

The lineup for 1966 is as follows:

Body	
#63A	Two-Door Fastback—Standard
#63B	Two-Door Fastback—Luxury
#65A	Two-door Hardtop—Standard
#65B	Two-Door Hardtop—Luxury
#65C	Two-Door Hardtop—Bench Seats
#75A	Convertible—Standard
#76B	Convertible—Luxury
#76C	Convertible—Bench Seats

1966 model year production totaled 607,568 with the three body styles. Buyers made the two-door hardtop in standard form the most popular model with 422,416 built, and convertible buyers

The '66's have a somewhat neater front grille appearance with the absence of the large bars flanking the Mustang emblem and a new grille background of bright metal bars. Ford also added the bright metal molding to the lip of the hood.

chose the bench seat model the least with 3,190 built. Production of fastbacks in 1966 dropped an unexplainable 46% with 27,809 produced as Body #63A and 7,889 as Body #63B. Convertible production, however, remained at a healthy total of 72,119 with 12,520 of this amount having the luxury interior decor group.

The convertible was the highest priced Mustang in base form in the lineup—$2,558—but $56 cheaper than last year. The fastback remained at the same price—$2,533—with the basic six-cylinder engine, but still suffered the significant drop in sales. The base price of the two-door hardtop was lowered $47 to $2,321 FOB Detroit. Standard equipment looked very similar to 1965 with wall-to-wall carpeting, floor-mounted stick shift, three-speed manual transmission, padded instrument panel, sun visors, vinyl upholstery, front arm rests (now padded), fresh air heater/defroster, windshield wipers, bucket seats, full stainless wheel covers (newly designed), sports steering wheel, automatic courtesy lights, cigarette lighter, glove box light, wrap-around front bumper, bumper guards front and rear, and the 200 CID in-line six-cylinder engine. Backup lights also became standard in 1966 as well as rear seat belts added to front seat belts Ford offered in 1965.

The fastback, of course, contained the extra standard features of a tinted rear window, functional side louvers, and the fold-down rear seat for extra carrying capacity. The convertible added the five-ply, vinyl-bonded top in back, white, or tan with a zip-out window and a matching stretch taut boot to stow the top.

OPTION LIST PASSES 100

At the beginning of the model year, Mustang brochures boasted over 70 items for its option list; but through the year dealer-installed option/accessories expanded the list to well over 100. Although a two-door hardtop retailed in base form for under the $2,500 level, most buyers ordered enough optional equipment to run the price tag into the $2,800 − $2,900 category. The following list gives one an idea of the price of some popular options:

Vinyl Roof	$74.36
Disc Brakes	56.77
Power Steering	84.47
Limited-Slip Differential	41.60

A 1966 convertible with the optional-styled steel wheels and accent paint stripe. Note the deluxe interior with the pony seats.

AM Radio	57.51
Air Conditioning	310.90
Automatic Transmission	185.39
Four-Speed Transmission	184.02
Rally-Pac	69.30
GT Equipment Group	152.20
Stereosonic Tape System	128.49
Tinted Glass	30.25
Whitewall Tires	33.31

FOUR ENGINES INCLUDE ONE SIX

For 1966, Mustangs are powered by four different factory original engines. Since Ford Division dropped the 170-cubic-inch six during the 1964/65 run, the 200 CID in-line six remained the standard powerplant listed for each of the three body styles. Having seven main bearings, the ohv-6 is rated a top 120 horsepower at 4400 rpm. It has a 9.2:1 compression ratio and uses a single one-barrel carburetor. The three-speed Cruise-O-Matics use a 2.83 rear axle ratio while the basic three-speed manual and optional four-speed shift utilize the 3.20 ratio. The six-cylinder continued to use its own fully synchronized four-speed transmission.

With the 260 dropped early in the 1965 model year, the V-8's appearing in '66 models are one of the three 289's. Many buyers chose the famous 289 two-barrel with a 200 horsepower output at 4400 rpm. This engine uses regular fuel with its 9.3:1 compression ratio and offers excellent gas mileage with the 2.80 rear axle ratio available with three transmissions—Cruise-O-Mastic, three-speed manual (synchronized on V-8's), and the four-speed manual. The engine is powerful enough in the lightweight Mustang for quick acceleration from a standstill even with the high speed 2.80 gears. Most cars equipped with this engine still run strong at 100,000 miles.

THE HOTTER V-8S AS BEFORE

A more powerful V-8 offered in 1966 is the 225 horsepower 289 similar to the previous engine with a higher compression ratio of 10.0:1 (premium fuel recommended) and using a four-barrel carburetor. The 3.00 gears were available with the standard three-speed manual, the optional three-speed automatic, or the optional four-speed manual.

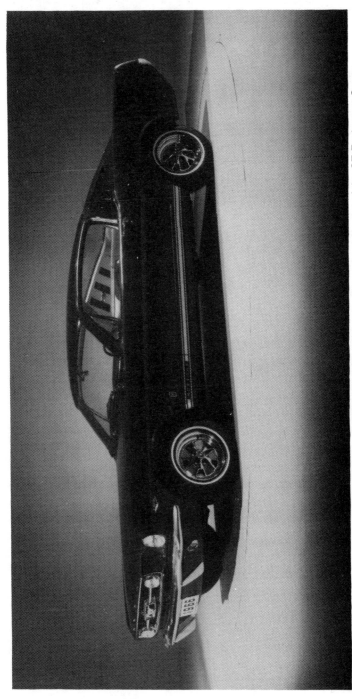

This 1966 fastback with GT trim is difficult to tell from a 1965 because of the grille bars added as part of the GT Equipment Group.

Another four-barrel 289, the high performance version with mechanical camming, returned for a second year in 1966 in similar form to 1965. Certainly not a great many of these expensive 271 horsepower engines were sold in 1965 or 1966. The high performance seeker in 1966 likely chose a Chevrolet Chevelle SS with 360 horsepower Turbo Jet 396 or a Pontiac GTO with the 360 horsepower tri-powered 389 cubic incher.

The high performance 289 continued to use its own four-speed transmission with closer ratio than that mated to other V-8's, but added the three-speed manual and Cruise-O-Matic. The automatic used the 3.50 gears, while the manual three-speed and four-speed used the 3.89's. Optional gear ratios were the 3.50's and the low speed 4.11's. When the optional Rally-Pace (tachometer and clock mounted in a twin-pod housing on top of the steering wheel) was ordered with this engine, its tachometer read from 0 to 8000 rpm rather than 0 to 6000 rpm.

MINOR CHANGES DISTINGUISH MODEL YEAR

The 1966 Mustang offers the famous looks of the original 65's by using the same body and chassis dimensions plus minor styling refinements that distinguish it from the earlier cars. Each body style has an overall length of 181.6 inches, a width of 68.2 inches, a height just over 51 inches, and a wheelbase of 108 inches. The width of the front track of the six-cylinder car is 55.4 inches and 56.0 inches for all models. Weight of the hardtop, fast-back, and convertible is 2606, 2636, and 2768 pounds respectively, with the standard equipment. All models have a fuel tank capacity of 16.0 gallons while the usable luggage capacity of the trunk of the hardtop, fastback, and convertible is 9.0, 7.2, and 5.0 cubic feet respectively.

On the outside, the most readily recognized styling refinement is the new look of the grille, unless the GT Equipment Group is ordered. The Mustang emblem and frame is minus the large horizontal bars and seems to float in the center of the grille mouth with a new background of bright, fine horizontal bars. The GT Mustangs of 1966, however, retain the large bars flanking the Mustang emblem, but are still distinguishable from the 65's with the new grille background that replaced the honeycomb pattern of metal in gun metal gray.

Pre-production cars for 1966 had a proposed three-lens design with each lens separated by about one inch and banded with chrome, as on this GT fastback. Note the "pop-open"-type filler cap characteristic of GT cars.

Other features of the GT cars include either the 225 or 271 horsepower V-8 engine requirement, dual exhausts with bright extensions through the rear panel, fog lamps, grille bar, disc brakes, special handling package, GT stripes, GT plaques, and GT fuel filler cap. Another styling refinement of '66's is the chrome molding around the lip of the hood just above the grille. The side scoop ornamentation (hardtop and convertible only) uses "windsplits" this year—three metal bars that have the look of channeling air flow to the rear wheels. Of course, the scoop is not functional. With the accent paint stripe, still available although not called a Tiffany stripe this year, the side scoop ornamentation is again deleted.

Other styling refinements include re-designed wheel covers and gas filler cap. The taillights are the same for 1966, although early pre-production cars had a proposed three-lens design with each lens separated by about one inch and banded with chrome. Ford dropped this design in favor of the previous "tri-port" scheme probably because each taillight then needed but one lens. Back-up lamps also became standard on 1966 models and are located in the lower panel below the rear bumper.

LOTS OF NEW '66 OPTIONS

The 16 exterior colors possible were joined by a wide variety of extra cost option/accessories. Examples of factory-installed items on the exterior included a convertible power-operated top, tinted glass for all windows, tinted glass for the windshield only, a rear-deck mounted luggage rack, vinyl roof covering in black or white, deluxe wheel covers, wire wheel covers, or styled wheel covers.

An unusual example of a dealer-installed accessory is the illuminated Mustang grille emblem which, when installed, replaces the chromed galloping Mustang horse (also seen in '65). Other gadgets included air horns, door-edge guards, doorsill plate, license plate frame, locking gas cap, lake pipes, engine/trunk compartment light, roof-mounted luggage rack kit, outside rear-view mirror (circular), remote control outside rear view mirror available with matching right non-remote mirror, racing stripes in red, white, or blue, radiator insect screen, reflector flare kit, ski rack kit, spotlight, tire chains, tonneau cover, tool kit, fender-mounted turn signals, wheel trim rings, and more added throughout the year.

STANDARD PANEL BETTER, BETTER SEATS OPTIONAL

On the inside, the most welcome change had to be the addition of the '65 GT instrument cluster to all '66 model cars. Five round dials placed in front of the driver show fuel level, oil pressure, speed, amperage, and water temperature. Formerly, the '65 Mustangs without the GT option used warning lights for oil pressure and water temperature.

The extremely durable vinyl bucket seats were still standard on '66's, and very popular. Although both front buckets are adjustable forward and backward and offer ample leg room even for six-footers, the seats are tiring after a couple hours drive.

The interior decor group, however, offers a softer more comfortable seat, wood-grained dash and steering wheel, door panels with molded arm rests, and courtesy/warning lights in the side of the door—making up the luxury interior. Of course, the tiny rear seats of the Mustangs of '65 and '66 offer little leg room. Rear seats of fastbacks give even less room, but the rear seat can be folded down to add more carrying capacity to the trunk, which also gives the car a sportier two-seater look.

Factory-installed interior option/accessories included air conditioning (still looking like an add-on positioned under the center of the dash), AM radio/stereosonic tape system, console, heater/defroster as a delete option, transistorized AM pushbutton radio with antenna, Rally-Pac, deluxe front and rear seat belts with front seat retractors and reminder light, full width front seat with center arm rest, deluxe steering wheel, and more.

Dealer-installed accessories produced some exotic possibilities with items like the CB radio, rear seat arm rests, clothes rod, compass, door storage compartment, fire extinguisher, floor mats, glove compartment and console door lock, rear seat light, parking brake warning light, 12-volt map light, litter basket, day/nite rearview mirror, conventional or studiosonic rear seat radio speaker, seat belt retractors, child's safety seat, ventilated seat cushion, stereosonic tape system, 6000 and 9000 rpm tachometers, tissue dispenser, tonneau cover for convertibles, remote trunk release lever, and more.

SUSPENSION THE SAME: NEEDS HELP

Handling characteristics of the '66 Mustangs parallel that of the '65's. Independent coil springs enclose the front shock absorbers mounted on top of the upper ball joints and provide good independent front suspension. The rear suspension, however, with the rear axle anchored by the leaf springs alone, takes away much from the handling characteristics of the Mustang. On rough roads, for example, the rear is apt to bounce from side to side. Quick acceleration from a standstill can easily result in the tires breaking adhesion.

Rear suspension is improved in several ways. The most common method is the addition of aftermarket traction bars. The special handling package, available on all V-8 cars, offered the heavy-duty front and rear springs, heavy-duty shock absorbers, larger diameter front stabilizer bar, and 21.7:1 steering ratio. The heavy-duty springs not only help keep the heavier V-8's from "bottoming out" on rough roads, but set the car slightly higher above the ground for a better performance look.

Power steering is a desirable option on V-8's but hardly necessary on the lighter steering sixes. Power brakes again were not listed in combination with the discs. The limited-slip differential, often called posi-track, was a good buy at just over forty dollars and recommended as part of a production option for cars that towed trailers weighing one to two thousand pounds.

SHELBY GT-350 AGAIN AND THE RENT-A-RACER

For the 1966 model year, Carroll Shelby again applied his racing experience to a stripped down version of the fastback to produce 2,500 GT-350 machines in Los Angeles, California. Of these, 936 were Hertz, 350-H models, three were "R" or competition models, and six were convertibles.

Shelby especially built the 350-H cars for the Hertz Rent-A-Car people who advertised it for rental coast-to-coast in the Hertz Sports Car Club. Leased in over 60 cities, the 350-H was easily identifiable with its black body and twin gold rally stripes extending from grille to rear bumper. This car quickly gained a reputation as the Hertz "Rent-a-Racer." A person could actually rent the 350-H, drive to the drag strip, win his class, and return the car to Hertz the same day.

Characteristic of the whole model year, changes are not great in the limited production of the GT-350, but are more aptly described as compromises to the '65's all-out sports car features. Exterior colors expanded to include red and green in addition to the one color

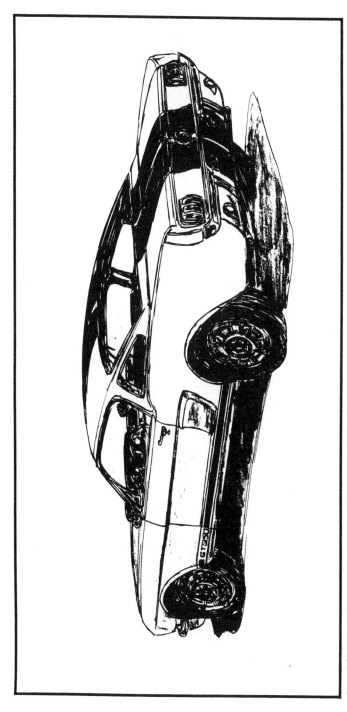

Carroll Shelby sold 2,500 of the Mustang GT-350's in its first full model year, 1966. That total includes a big order of over 900 cars bought by the Hertz Rent-A-Car people. Rear plexiglass windows replaced the functional side louvers of the '65's for a more stylish look.

seen in '65—Wimbleton White. Shelby made automatic transmission optional in 1966 and moved the noisy Detroit "No Spin" differential to the option list with the 3.89's standard. Rear plexiglass quarter windows replaced the functional side louvers of the '65's for a more stylish look, and Shelby added functional side scoops to the '66's.

1967:

New Styling and Rivals Arrive

For 1967, Mustang underwent its first major styling change as Ford Motor Company encountered its first challenging competition in the specialty, personal car field. The Chevrolet Camaro, Mercury Cougar, Pontiac Firebird, and Plymouth Barracuda joined the Mustang in the new ponycar field with stylish new bodies that used the long nose, short deck theme. Production figures reveal the Mustang as the most popular, as follows:

1967 Model Year Production

Ford Mustang	472,121
Chevrolet Camaro	220,906
Mercury Cougar	150,893
Pontiac Firebird	82,560
Plymouth Barracuda	62,534

Even with production down about one-fifth from the previous year, Mustang sold more than double that of the Camaro, the closest rival. Lincoln-Mercury Division of Ford complemented Mustang's total with over 150,000 of the luxury Cougars. Also, total industry sales dropped in 1967; however, Mustang remained unmistakably number one in the ponycar field.

NEW BODY STYLES LEAD LINEUP

Ford continued to offer the Mustang in hardtop, convertible, and fastback, but gave the cars completely re-shaped exteriors, a new instrument panel configuration, and improved suspension arrangement, added safety features, and more. The lineup with respect to body numbers consisted of the following:

Body	
#63A	Two-Door Fastback—Standard
#63B	Two-Door Fastback—Luxury
#65A	Two-Door Hardtop—Standard
#65B	Two-Door Hardtop—Luxury
#65C	Two-Door Hardtop—Bench Seats
#76A	Convertible—Standard
#76B	Convertible—Luxury
#76C	Convertible—Bench Seats

The most popular body style continued to be the two-door hardtop with production topping the 350,000 mark. For $2,461, standard equipment included the 200 CID six-cylinder, a fully synchronized three-speed manual transmission, all-vinyl interior, full carpeting, courtesy lighting, cigarette lighter, ash tray, sports steering wheel, reversible keys, keyless locking, suspended accelerator pedal (nothing new), heater/defroster, remote control outside rearview mirror, and bumper guards.

Each model contained what Ford called "Lifeguard Design Safety Features." These consist of a dual hydraulic brake system with a dash-mounted warning light, impact-absorbing steering wheel with deep padded hub, four-way emergency flasher, lane changer turn signal, remote control outside rearview mirror, double-yoke safety door latches and hinges to help keep doors shut on impact, door lock buttons that must be raised to open the door from inside, thick laminate safety plate glass, padded windshield pillars, padded sun visors, padded insturment panel, front and rear seat belts with retractors for the front seat passengers, day/night inside mirror with breakaway support or double pivot support, two-speed or variable speed windshield wipers, windshield washers, backup lights, front seat shoulder harness anchors, safety rim wheels, corrosion-resistant brake lines, safety-designed instrument panel

Mustang underwent its first major styling change in 1967, but managed to retain the look of the first cars. The grille consumes the entire space between the bumper and the hood this year, and the grille bars returned.

and controls, uniform shift quadrant, reduced-glare instrument panel—wiper arms—blades, and energy-absorbing steering wheel.

In addition to the above standard equipment, the convertible and fastback offered extras with a base price of $2,698 and $2,592, respectively. Fastback sales rebounded dramatically with over 53,000 produced in standard form and over 17,000 made with the luxury trim. Extras on the fastback consisted of the full-sweep tinted glass back window, Silent-Flo Ventilation for fresh air with the windows up via the functional side louvers, and full wheel covers. Production of convertibles, although still very healthy with sales near the 45,000 level, began a slide that would persist until its last year of availability in 1973. Its extras included the five-play, vinyl-bonded top with zip-out window and matching stretch taut boot to stow the top.

ARRIVAL OF THE BIG BLOCK 390

The engine lineup for 1967 is identical to 1966 except for the addition of the highly-welcomed big block 390. Ford again used the 200-cubic-inch in-line six as standard for each model and offered the 289 in the same three versions—the ever popular two-barrel, the four-barrel, and for the final season sold the high-revving, high-performance, solid lifter, 271 horsepower four-barrel.

The addition of the 390 to the stable added a muscle car to the Mustang lineup. It also helped obsolete the expensive 271 horse-power "Cobra-type" 289. The later engine retailed for an extra $327.92, while the 320 horsepower 390 cost $158.08 additional.

As could be expected, a few high-performance 289's sold as most performance-minded buyers wanting a small block engine chose the much cheaper ($52.85 extra) 225 horsepower 289 which they hopped up with Cobra speed accessories. The 390, a member of the 352/390/428 family of Ford engines and first sold in 1961, was nothing new; but it was quite unexpected in the little Mustang. The 390 cleared way for the extra space needed within the engine compartment to drop a 427 or 428 with a minimum of cutting and fabricating.

MANY VIRTUES OF THE 390

The 390 with standard Holley four-barrel carburetor, bore and stroke of 4.050 × 3.784 inches, and 10.5:1 compression ratio, gen-

The panel above the rear bumper of the 1967's is concave rather than slightly convex as in the past, and the taillights went to a three-lens configuration similar to the one proposed in 1966.

erates 320 horsepower at 3600 rpm running on premium gasoline. This engine uses hydraulic valve lifters and a mild yet effective cam that creates the quiet operation and easy maintenance. With four-speed transmission and standard high-speed 3.00 gears, the 390 Mustang can run the standing start quarter mile in about 15 seconds at about 95 mph. And then the performance enthusiast had lots of over-the-counter speed parts for added go, like cast-iron headers, three two-barrel and dual four-barrel manifold kits, Rally Pacs, Air Lift kits, etc. Also available with the 390 was the new Select Shift Cruise-O-Matic automatic transmission and optional gear ratios of 2.80, 3.25, and 3.50.

SELECT SHIFT SIMULATES MANUAL SHIFT

The new Select Shift, standard on all Cruise-O-Matics, uses a standard shift quadrant with six positions arranged with the following manner: P-R-N-D-2-1. In the normal driving position D, the transmission starts in low and upshifts to second and high. In Drive 2, the transmission starts in second and remains in second gear until the selector is moved. In low, of course, the transmission remains in low gear. This arrangement allows for manual shifting of gears simulating a three-speed manual. The driver can start in low, wind the engine to the desired rpm, shift to Drive 2, wind the engine to "x" rpm's again, and then push the selector to high.

MANY 1967 STYLING CHANGES

With respect to exterior styling, the body surface of the '67's is completely reshaped, but the car resembles the original Mustang.

The height of the grille mouth is larger, consuming the entire space between the front bumper and the hood. The Mustang emblem in the center of the grille is flanked by large bars set against a background of tiny metal rectangles. In the past, the vertical bumper guards set against the panel below the bumper were made of bright metal. For 1967, the rear bumper guards are colored the same as the body with inserts of gray rubber, while the front bumper guards are bright metal with rubber inserts. The characteristic Mustang side sculpturing on the 67's is more pronounced than in the past with twin-simulated air scoops just ahead of the rear wheel cutouts. The panel above the rear bumper is concave rather than slightly convex

The interior of a 1967 model with Select Shift Cruise-O-Matic, air conditioning with in-dash registers, brushed aluminum instrument panel applique, console with AM radio and tape player, a vertical lighted storage compartment with sliding door, and seat belts with retractors.

as in the past. The taillights to either side of this panel went to three-lens configuration with each lens separated by about one inch and banded with bright metal. The gas cap, with appropriate identification, is also positioned in the center of the panel for easy fueling.

The all-new body shell of the fastback features a full-length fastback roof for the first time in 1967 rather than the three-quarter effect of 1965 and 1966.

When the custom exterior trim group is ordered, each body style takes on a slightly different look. The gap caps have a "pop-open" lever, the hood is louvered to accommodate turn signals visible to the driver, the wheel openings have bright metal moldings as do the rear decklids and quarter panels, plus lower back panel grilles on fastbacks.

OPTIONS DELUGE CONTINUES

The GT Equipment Group of 1967 was available for all models with V-8 engines and included four-inch driving lamps at each end of the horizontal grille bar, F70-14 Wide-Oval WSW tires, GT racing stripes and ornamentation, GT pop-open gas cap, power disc brakes, heavy-duty suspension (the special handling package), plus dual exhaust system with bright "quad" extensions on the 390 and 289 high-performance V-8.

The convertible introduced a new option with a unique back glass, hinged horizontally in the middle with a clear rubber strip that allowed the window to double on itself when the top was lowered. This window on '67 soft tops is a very desirable option since the top can be lowered without having to un-zip the rear plastic window.

Other exterior factory option/accessories included tinted glass for all windows, rear-deck-mounted luggage rack kit, accent stripe, two-tone paint for the back panel that used dark metallic gray in combination with the body color, a protection group that consisted of color-keyed floor mats in front and rear, door-edge guards, license plate frames front and rear, and a vinyl roof for the hardtop in black or pastel parchment.

Dealer-installed option/accessories consisted of an assortment of extras not unlike that found in any popular parts store catalog. The most interesting one perhaps is the illuminated Mustang grille emblem, sometimes called the lighted horse.

DIMENSIONS UP ALL AROUND

With respect to dimensions and capacities, the '67's are a bit longer, wider, and taller. The length grew two inches from 181.6 to 183.6 inches; the width increased significantly from 68.2 inches to 70.9 inches; and the height added about one-half inch overall. The curb weight varied from 2,695 pounds for a six-cylinder hardtop to 3,045 pounds for a convertible with the 390 V-8. Trunk luggage volume remained virtually the same despite increased overall dimensions. Hardtop, convertible (top down), and fastback capacity

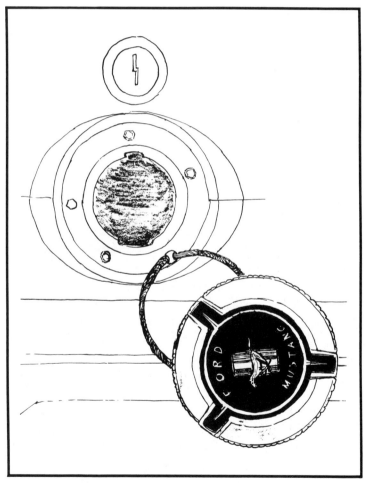

The screw-off gas cap of the Mustang is secured by a wire. This unique cap with Mustang identification further adds to the personal character of the car.

equals 9.2, 7.7, and 5.1 cubic feet respectively. Wheelbase remained the familiar 108 inches. Cars with the 289 engines has a gas tank capacity of 17 gallons while the six-cylinder and 390 CID V-8's have a 16-gallon capacity.

MANY VARIATIONS OF NEW PANEL

On the inside, the instrument panel underwent the biggest change from the previous year and gives several different looks with the options available. Two larger circular dials flanked above by three smaller circular dials house a full set of standard gauges—speedometer, plus fuel, temperature, oil pressure, and alternator gauges. Curiously, when one orders the tachometer and trip odometer that appears in the large dial on the right, he gets warning lights for the alternator and oil pressure plus a clock in the center dial. This tachometer reads to a maximum 6,000 rpm except with the high-performance 289 which reads to 8,000 rpm.

INTERIOR OPTIONS IN PROFUSION

An interior decor option (deluxe model car) included molded door trim panels, padded quarter trim panels (hardtop only), courtesy/warning light in doors, grille on door lower panels, roof console with map lights (hardtop and fastback), bright trim on foot pedals, brushed aluminum instrument panel appliques, vinyl cover "T" shift lever, bright buttons in seat backs, special ornamentation, and an electric clock.

Also, an optional convenience panel that required a console when ordered with Select Aire air conditioning gave the buyer of either hardtop, fastback, or convertible a satin-brushed aluminum panel with door ajar warning light, parking brakes light, low fuel warning light, and seat belt light. The new Select Aire air conditioning provided dash-mounted air registers for the first time in the Mustang. The under-dash-mounted air conditioning system, however, was still available but relegated to a dealer-installed accessory, and the heater still a delete option.

An interesting option console carried the AM radio, a vertical-lighted storage compartment with sliding door, and the gearshift. A tilt/swing steering wheel was also available on the Mustang for the first time. By pushing the turn signal lever forward, the wheel tilts to

A new option on the convertible this year is the unique back glass, hinged horizontally in the middle with a clear rubber strip that allowed the window to double on itself when lowered. Note the lower back panel grille, pop-open-type gas cap, and styled steel wheels.

any one of nine positions. With the transmission in park, the motor not running, the wheel moves 45 degrees to the right when the door is opened.

A courtesy light group for all models consisted of under-hood luggage compartment lights and a glove box light with hardtops that included an under-dash and courtesy light.

Other factory-installed interior option/accessories included the AM/FM push-button radio, stereosonic tape system (AM radio required), front seat belt shoulder harness, rear seat sport deck option on fastback (the fixed rear seat is standard on the fastback for the first time in 1967), fingertip speed control for cars with V-8's and Cruise-O-Matic, ventilated (comfortweave) vinyl trim on the hardtop and fastback except with the bench seat, deluxe steering wheel, and console (radio required).

With respect to dealer-installed option/accessories, the novelty of the CB radio, also available for this year, was surpassed by an optional 9-inch television set with antenna and hanging bracket.

ALL CHASSIS MOUNTS RUBBER-BUSHED

Suspension and accompanying handling characteristics improved slightly for 1967. Of importance is the fact that all contact points between the suspension components and the chassis are rubber-bushed starting this year. Also, although the front and rear suspension are basically the same with independent coil in front and leaf spring in the rear, the front uses a re-engineered front-end geometry with lower upper arm pivots. Rear suspension retains the "asymetrical variable rate design with rear axle located forward of spring centers" and diagonally-mounted shock absorbers.

Steering, of the same recirculating-ball type with steering gear and permanently-lubricated steering linkage joints, now uses an overall manual steering ratio of 25.4:1 and an overall power steering ratio of 20.3:1.

SIGNIFICANT BRAKE IMPROVEMENTS

With respect to brakes, 1967 Mustangs use for the first time a dual hydraulic system that begins with a dual master cylinder under the hood. Separate lines run from each cylinder to the front and rear wheels; and in the event one side of the system malfunctions, the

For the first time, the Mustang fastback featured a full-length fastback roof, as on this 1967 GT fastback, rather than the three-quarter effect of 1965 and 1966. Overall sales of fastbacks about doubled from the previous year.

One of the most interesting Mustang options (offered since 1965), had to be the illuminated Mustang grille emblem, sometimes called the "lighted horse."

other side of the cylinder can stop the car. A red warning light on the dash lights when any half of the brake system malfunctions. Power disc brakes are available for the first time this year, while power drum brakes became a dealer-installed option.

HD AND COMPETITION SUSPENSION PACKS

A heavy-duty suspension costing about $30 extra provided V-8 cars with stiffer springs and shock absorbers, plus a larger diameter front stabilizer bar. Ford also sold on a limited production basis a competition handling package for GT cars powered by either the 289 high-performance or the 390 CID engine. This competition handling package sounds like something borrowed from one of Shelby's Mustangs. For almost $400, this rare option offered a very stiff suspension consisting of extra stiff front and rear springs, adjustable shock absorbers, extra heavy stabilizer bar, 16:1 overall ratio steering gear, high ratio rear axle with unique wheel covers, six-inch wide rims, and 6.50/6.70 × 15 sports car nylon tires.

SHELBY GT-500 JOINS GT-350

For 1967, production of the Shelbys moved to Detroit, and luxury features continued to crowd the performance equipment of the car. Power brakes and power steering, for example, became mandatory. The GT-350 was joined by the GT-500 with either a 427 or 428 CID big block engine. Ford sold 1,175 of the GT-350 with the high-performance, Shelby-prepared 289 and 2,050 of the GT-500's.

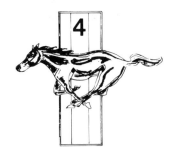

1968:

First Among Muscle Cars

After a complete restyling for 1967 when Mustang met its first real competition and remained the undisputed leader of the newly-outlined ponycar field, Ford again offered the hardtop, fastback, and convertible with minor modifications for 1968.

The American Motors Javelin joined the Mustang, Camaro, Courgar, Firebird, and Barracuda as the newest ponycar. Intermediate-sized specialty cars emerged as a group and penetrated ponycar sales to some extent. These cars, such as the Oldsmobile 4-4-2, Pontiac GTO, Plymouth Roadrunner, Ford Torino GT, and others combined performance and sporty looks in a larger, heavier package.

Although the gap between Mustang and its nearest rival, the Chevrolet Camaro, narrowed, Mustang still led in production and popularity by over 80,000 units. It's no surprise that changes to the Mustang are minimal this year; and it takes a second look to tell a 1967 from a 1968 model.

BODIES SIMILAR BUT BIG NEW ENGINES

Under the hood, however, the engine lineup was considerably beefed with the addition of the 427 and 428 CJ big block power houses. The 428 Cobra Jet, added to the engine list in mid-model year, gave the Mustang a firm supercar status and a top position in the muscle car field. Of this engine *Hot Rod* magazine stated:

> "The Cobra Jet will be the utter delight of every Ford lover and the bane of all the rest because, quite frankly, it is the fastest running Pure Stock in the history of man."

Ford re-quoted this statement in an ad appearing in performance magazines in the spring of 1968 and offered the engine in all Ford Fairlanes, Torinos, and Mustang GT's. The model year line-up consisted of the following:

Body

#63A	Two-Door Fastback—Standard
#63B	Two-Door Fastback—Deluxe
#63C	Two-Door Fastback—Bench Seats
#63D	Two-Door Fastback—Deluxe Bench Seats
#65A	Two-Door Hardtop—Standard
#65B	Two-Door Hardtop—Deluxe
#65C	Two-Door Hardtop—Bench Seats
#65D	Two-Door Hardtop—Deluxe Bench Seats
#76A	Convertible—Standard
#76B	Convertible—Deluxe

For the first time one could order a bench seat in a fastback. Also for the first time, a person could specify a car (deluxe) with bench seats—one with the interior decor group. The combination of a fastback body style and a bench seat made for a rare car; however, a deluxe fastback with a bench seat made for an even more unlikely partnership. Out of over 40,000 fastbacks, Ford put together a mere 256 of Body #63D. Convertible production dropped considerably in 1968—over 40%!—while hardtops remained the most popular.

MANY FORMER EXTRAS NOW STANDARD

Standard features on the '68's sounded familiar. The 200 CID in-line six remained the standard powerplant for the three body styles, while Ford offered for a second year a fully-synchronized, three-speed manual transmission at no extra cost. Buyers again chose exterior color from sixteen "Brilliant Super Diamond Lustre Enamel Finishes," and selected from a total of 40 all-vinyl interiors in eight different colors. Other standard features included the

The 1968's look very similar to the 1967 cars. The grille of the '68 is more deeply inset this year, and the grille bars again disappeared as part of styling refinements.

individually-adjustable deep-foam bucket seats, 100% nylon loop pile carpeting, courtesy lighting, cigarette lighter and ash tray, reversible keys, "keyless" locking, suspended accelerator pedal, heater/defroster, curved side glass, outside rearview mirror, center fill fueling, bright decklid and quarter panel extension moldings, rocker panel molding, anodized aluminum scuff plates, floor-mounted shift lever with all transmissions, coat hooks, dual sun visors, "Twice-a-Year" maintenance, and the Standard Ford Motor Company Lifeguard Design Safety Features. These features included those for 1967 plus side marker lights or reflectors, energy absorbing front seat back tops with padding, self-locking folding seats, shoulder belts for outboard front seat passengers (except convertibles), vehicle structure designed to limit steering column displacement, safety-designed coat hooks, safety-designed window regulator knobs, safety-designed radio push buttons, and windshield-mounted rearview mirror.

The base price of the hardtop with these standard features amounted to $2,602, which is less than $300 more than the original car that debuted in 1964. And the 1968 model contains a host of extra standard equipment. Obviously, Ford re-invested profits from the sale of the immensely popular earlier cars in an effort to keep Mustang number one.

The fastback retailed in base form for $2,712, or less than $200 more than the original fastback introduced in the fall of 1964. The fastback again used the roof quarter panel air outlets to provide what Ford called "Silent-Flo Ventilation" and a full sweep-tinted glass back window. The convertible ($2,814), included a five-ply vinyl top with a boot to match the color of the interior. The boot should not be confused with the optional tonneau cover, the later of which stretches over the interior of the car when the top is down. The boot fits over the lowered top by way of concealed fasteners. The back window of the convertible is made of clear vinyl and should be zipped out before lowering the top.

MOST POWER TRAIN CHOICES SO FAR

For 1968, a buyer had a wide range of engine choices and accompanying powertrain with a total of seven engines, four transmissions, and nine rear axle ratios. The six cylinder 200 CID engine,

The limited production "California Special" with Shelby-like side scoops, taillights, side stripping and pop-open-type gas cap.

rated at 115 horsepower at 3,800 rpm was a familiar engine used since 1965. Its main asset was delivering over 20 miles per gallon with its 8.8:1 compression ratio, single one-barrel carburetor, standard three-speed transmission, and moderate 3.20 rear axle ratio. The optional Cruise-O-Matic transmission used 2.83 gears as standard with the 3.20's optional.

The famous 289 all-purpose V-8's that became virtually synonymous with the name Mustang were installed in Mustangs for the last time in model year 1968. Ford sold but one version of this engine, the low-compression (8.7:1), single two-barrel, which delivered 195 horsepower at 4,600 rpm. The three-speed transmission and 2.79 gears were common with the 289. Automatic and four-speeds, plus 2.79 or 3.00 gear ratios teamed with the 289 also.

NEW 302 V-8 JOINS THE LINEUP

The next larger volume engine mounted in 1968 Mustangs was the 302 cubic-inch V-8, new this year. Dimensionally, the 302 is the 289 with a slightly longer stroke of 3.00 inches and the same bore of 4.00 inches. Like the 289, it uses the stud-mounted rockers, wedge-shaped combustion chambers, etc. Called the Challenger Special V-8 by Ford, the 302's standard transmission was the three-speed manual with optional Select Shift Cruise-O-Matic and four-speed manual. With each transmission, 3.00 gears are common, with 3.25 optional.

The 390, first offered in 1967 in a performance-oriented four-barrel, emerged this year in two and four-barrel forms. The four-barrel, called the 390 GT or Thunderbird Special V-8, provided 335 horsepower at 4,800 rpm. It used premium fuel with its 10.5:1 compression ratio. Available with each of the three transmissions, standard gears are the 3.00's with the 3.25's optional. The new two-barrel 390, called the Thunderbird V-8, developed 265 horsepower at 4,400 rpm with a 9.5:1 compresison ratio that allowed the burning of regular fuel. The buyer of the 390-2V had to purchase the optional automatic transmission if he wanted this engine.

427 AND 428 BIG BLOCKS WEDGED IN

Ford dropped two more big cube monsters into the Mustang in model year 1968—the 427 and 428 CJ. For a car weighing around

From this angle the '68 looks very similar to a '67. But the '68's use side marker lights on the front and rear quarter panels as part of the Ford Lifeguard Design Safety Features.

3,000 pounds and resting on a 108-inch wheelbase, the Mustang was getting a lot of engine crammed under its hood. The 427 "Wedge," first developed for racing and introduced in the 1964 Ford lineup, rated 390 horsepower at 5,400 rpm, burned premium fuel with 10.9:1 compression ratio, and like the 390-2V was listed available with the extra cost automatic transmission only. A major attribute of the 427 block is the five main bearings with the center three cross-bolted for extra strength and durability. Camming is hydraulic in the 1968 427; bore and stroke equals 4.236 × 3.781 inches; and like the other large cube engines, it gives high torque to low rpm—an incredible 460-foot pounds at 3,200 rpm! But the 427 saw limited production in the Mustang, and the average performance enthusiast could not realize its high-performance capacities. Ford dropped production of the 427 altogether after this year.

The 428 CJ, introduced in mid-model year in Cobra Jet (improved performance) form, drew high interest from the average performance buyer. Bore and stroke of the 428 CJ equalled 4.130 × 3.984 inches with a compression ratio of 10.5:1. This engine, with a smaller bore and longer stroke than the 427 (which computes the similar volume), combined with the lower compression ratio to make for a more docile engine in normal traffic. Camming is hydraulic, the block is constructed of cast nodular iron like the 427 for high strength, the new cylinder heads use huge ports actually bigger than the ones on the 427 racing heads, and large intake and exhaust valves measure 2.097 and 1.660 inches respectively!

Although Ford rated the stock CJ at a "conservative" 335 horsepower, the NHRA figured it at over 400. The figure is indeed conservative as the basic 428 rated five more horsepower. The 428 CJ made a top super stocker on the dragstrip with other high-performance equipment—like lightweight valves, high-ratio rocker arms, solid lifter cams, etc. Automatic and four-speed manual transmission with standard 3.50 gears and optional 3.25's were available with the CJ. The three speed, of course, made little sense to a buyer ordering this engine and was not available.

STYLING CHANGES DISTINGUISH MODEL

For 1968, Mustangs received minor styling changes and differ from 1967 models with several exteriors. The grille of the 1968 is

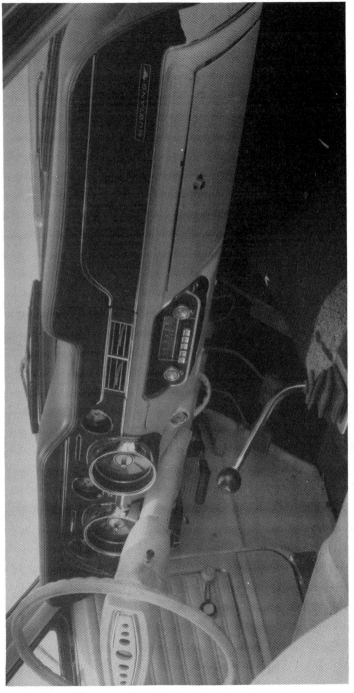

The basic interior configuration of a 1968 model with two-spoke steering wheel, three-speed manual transmission, bench seat, etc. The foot pedal directly below the hand emergency brake works the windshield wipers.

more deeply inset with a chrome strip banding the outside edge of the grille background. The Mustang emblem and frame located in the center of the grille is smaller this year and is not flanked by the larger horizontal metal spears. As in 1967, however, GT-equipped cars carry the four-inch fog lights in each end of the grille. Front and rear side marker lights appeared in 1968 models for safety reasons. The pronounced side sculpturing characteristic of all Mustangs through 1968 uses a wide, single, simulated air scoop with a subtle dark metal molding, rather than the simulated twin-air scoops of 1967.

A reflective group included GT tape (in white, red, blue, black, or gold), and reflective paint on styled steel wheels, and was available with the GT Equipment Group only. Cars with the latter option, which could be any model with a V-8 engine (except for 289-2V), included a dual exhaust system with bright extensions, fog lamps, special GT ornamentation, six-inch wide rims with E70-14 Wide Oval WSW tires, heavy-duty suspension, painted GT wheels, chrome trim rings, pop-open gas filler cap, and chrome engine components on the 390, 427, and 428 V-8's.

DECOR, PAINT AND PROTECTION OPTIONS

A special decor group included some interior and some exterior appointments. Optional with all models, it consisted of a wood-grained instrument panel applique, two-tone painted hood, knitted vinyl inserts in bucket seats for the hardtop and fastback, bright wheel lip molding, and the extra features for V-8 cars of E70 Wide Oval WSW tires, and argent-painted, slotted-steel wheels with bright trim rings.

A two-tone paint option combined low gloss black paint on the top of the hood and cowl (with the body color).

The protection group consisted of color-keyed floor mats in front and rear, door-edge guards, and front and rear license plate frames.

The Ford block letters seen on the leading edge of all earlier Mustangs disappeared in 1968. The vinyl roof was still a factory item; but an interesting dealer-installed accessory was a spray-on "vinyl roof."

Other popular factory-installed option/accessories of interest are the power top for the convertible, then folding glass backlite for

The 1968 fastback with GT trim and the new side striping pattern of 1968.

the convertible, tinted glass for all windows, an accent stripe, and a first-time-offered rear window defogger.

Probably because of the immense popularity of the Mustang in California, Ford produced a limited production "California Special" hardtop in 1968. Approximately one of every five Mustangs produced in America were California-bound in the Sixties. This custom-type car featured Shelby-like side scoops (simulated), taillights, and side stripes. The car used appropriate lettering, GT/SC, and a rear deck spoiler integral with the trunk lid.

INTERIOR CHOICES UP TO LUXURY LEVEL

Interiors of the '68's parallel that of the '67's with very minor changes, most with safety in mind. Front seats, with extra thick seat back padding this year, use new seat back latches that must be disengaged to push the seat back forward. These latches keep the seats from flopping forward on quick stops and protect the rear seat passengers. Another new feature is the paddle-type inside door latches that must be folded down to open the door. Rearview mirrors are windshield-mounted for the first time this year. Steering wheels are of the two-spoke variety this year and padded, again with safety in mind.

The interior decor group, minus the electric clock this year, made a luxury car of any Mustang model with the following: two-tone door trim panels, padded quarter trim panels (hardtop only), red/white door courtesy lights, lower door grille, roof console with map lights (hardtop and fastback), bright trim on foot pedals, wood grain instrument panel appliques, vinyl-covered "T" shift lever (simulated wood grain knob with manual transmission), bright buttons in seat backs, and wood grain steering wheel rim and insert. Other factory interior features remain from last year, such as the five-pod instrument cluster with optional tachometer and trip odometer, the Select Aire air conditioning system with the four-panel air registers, sport deck option, tilt/swing steering wheel, console, deluxe steering wheel, electric clock, bucket seats with knitted vinyl, courtesy light group, convenience panel, deluxe seat and shoulder belts with reminder light, fingertip speed control, pushbutton AM radio, stereosonic tape system/AM radio, and more.

The first regular production Shelby convertible in GT-500 form. The padded steel overhead safety bar is standard.

A LITTLE MORE SUSPENSION ATTENTION

Good handling is characteristic of ponycars and Americans enjoyed Mustangs from the very beginning for their excellent roadability. Suspension plus accompanying ride and handling traits improved slightly in 1968. As in 1967, contact points between the suspension components and the platform frame/body unit use rubber bushings to dampen vibration which reduces noise. The front suspension of '68 models, however, has a curved lower strut control arm that lets the front wheels absorb the shock rather than the steering mechanism for improved ride.

The harsh competition handling package of '67 is not listed this year, but the heavy-duty suspension option consists of increased rate front and rear springs, larger front and rear shock absorbers, and larger diameter front stabilizer bar. But the handling of the stock Mustang is so satisfactory that the latter option is not as necessary as it was for the earlier cars—1964-65-66.

The floating caliper power front disc brakes and rear drums give the Mustang perhaps the best stopping ability in the ponycar field for 1968. The 390, 427, and 428 use the power discs up front because of the difficulty of their increased weight. Steering ratio with manual steering is 25.3:1 overall and quicker 20.3:1 with power assist. Although not really needed on the lighter steering sixes, power steering is a highly-desirable option with the big block V-8's or with cars using the wide oval tires.

Length of the 1968 Mustang is 183.6 inches; width is 70.9 inches; wheelbase is the familiar 108 inches; fuel capacity is 16 gallons; tread width is 58.5 inches. Usable trunk volume remained low with 9.3, 6.8, and 5.6 cubic feet for the hardtop, convertible, and fastback, respectively. The sport deck rear seat option, however, expanded carrying capacity of the fastback to 18.5 cubic feet with the rear seat folded down. Approximate weights varied from 2,758 pounds representing the six-cylinder hardtop to 3,076 for the V-8 convertible.

PEAK YEAR FOR SHELBYS

In 1968, production of Shelbys reached a peak with 4,450 produced. However, as Ford involved its regular production Mustang deeper into the performance, muscle car field and adopted features from the earlier Shelbys, a duplication of effort was beginning to take place; the Shelbys were even produced in Michigan. The GT-350 now used a 250-horsepower 302 CID engine with hydraulic lifters rather than the solid lifter 289 discontinued last year. The GT-500, produced in a competition version, used either the 427 or 428 engine and accounted for most of the production:

GT-350	Fastback	1,253
	Convertible	404
GT-500	Fastback	1,140
	Fastback (KR)	933 (Competition)
	Convertible	402
	Convertible (KR)	318 (Competition)

1969:
Major Changes and Ten Engines

For 1969, the Mustang: longer, wider, and heavier than any previous year with more models and engine options available in its past or future, 1964-1973. The model lineup expanded as the Mach I fastback, the Grande hardtop, and the mid-year-introduced supercars—the Boss 302 and Boss 429—completed the basic hardtop, convertible, and sportsroof (formerly called fastback).

An incredible array of ten engines powered these cars as Ford went wild in the performance department. With base prices of Mustangs nearing the $3,000 level, and over that mark for the Mach I and the Boss cars, Ford introduced in mid-model year 1969 the sporty looking Maverick at a base price under $2,000 on a 103-inch wheelbase with an overall length about the same as the original Mustang, 173.3".

Although comparisons were sure to be made, Ford tried to keep the Maverick in a different class than the Mustang so that it would not draw too many sales from the existing lineup. Thus, Mavericks of 1969 contained no power steering, disc brakes, or handling package options. In fact, none hid V-8 engines beneath their hoods. But, a shift to smaller cars in America was developing, and 1969 is the last really good year for ponycars with respect to production. Mustang recorded a mere 5.5% drop in total sales to 299,824. The Chevrolet Camaro, however, narrowed the gap again between itself and the leader, producing 243,085 of these increasingly popular cars. The Mustang lineup with respect to body number is as follows:

Body	
#63A	Two-Door Fastback—Standard
#63B	Two-Door Fastback—Deluxe
#63C	Two-Door Fastback—Mach I
#65A	Two-Door Handtop—Standard
#65B	Two-Door Hardtop—Deluxe
#65C	Two-Door Hardtop—Bench Seats
#65D	Two-Door Hardtop—Deluxe, Bench Seats
#65E	Two-Door Hardtop—Grande
#76A	Convertible—Standard
#76B	Convertible—Deluxe

MACH I LED FASTBACK BOOM

The Mach I sent production figures soaring for the fastback body style; production of fastbacks surpassed in total numbers that of any other year with over 134,000 built. The Mach I accounted for over 70,000 of those sales, while the deluxe version of the fastback could not sell quite 6,000 units. Even so, the hardtop remained the most popular choice with respect to body style, aided by over 20,000 of the newly-introduced Grandes.

The marketing trend that developed this year in the Mustang lineup was to sell options in package form and then give the car a distinctive name. This concept not only helped sell more options and accessories, but it gave the buyer a better price on the extra items he purchased, provided he really wanted them all. Convertible sales totaled less than 15,000.

STANDARD FEATURES RUNDOWN

The 1969 hardtop displayed a base retail price of $2,618 FOB Detroit and consisted of the following standard features: 200 CID six, floor-mounted shift lever, individually-adjustable bucket seats, nylon loop-pile carpeting, courtesy lighting, cigarette lighter, reversible keys, keyless locking, dual sun visors, coat hooks, inside and outside left-hand rearview mirrors, suspended pedals, heater/defroster, vinyl interior, anodized aluminum scuff plates, center fill

Ford called the fastback body style a sportsroof beginning in 1969. The '69's use dual headlights and a blackout-type grille.

fueling, Autolite sta-full battery, twice-a-year maintenance. Also, the curved side windows for 1969 are "ventless," tires are special profile, and headlamps use four beams paired horizontally. Lifeguard Design Safety Features are the same as 1968 with the addition of a safety-designed front end structure.

For another $231, the Grande sold the following extra equipment: special sound insulation package, special soft ride suspension, luxury cloth and vinyl seat trim, molded door panels with integral arm rests and safety/courtesy lights, wood-like three-spoke rim blow steering wheel, teak-toned instrument panel and cluster appliques, padded interior quarter trim panels with arm rests, electric clock, two-tone narrow tape stripe, wire-style wheel covers, wheel opening moldings, bright rear deck molding, rocker panel molding. and dual racing-style outside rearview mirror.

CONVERTIBLE & FASTBACK, STANDARDS & OPTIONS

The convertible sold in base form for $2,632 with the same standard features of the hardtop plus a five-ply vinyl top manually-operated with clear vinyl backlite, color-keyed boot, and easy-action top-fastening latches.

The sportsroof sold for $2,618 with several features not found in the hardtop. Ford added an integral rear deck spoiler, swing-out rear quarter window, and tinted glass for the rear window.

But, for $3,122, or $508 more than the standard sportsroof, the Mach I buyer received a barrel full of extra standard features. These included the new 351-2V V-8 engine, GT equipment group mechanical components, competition handling suspension, F70-14 wide oval white sidewall belted tires, black low-gloss paint on the hood and cowl, special sound insulation package, high-backed bucket seats, dual racing-type mirrors with remote control for driver's side, molded door trim panels with integral arm rest and safety courtesy lights, wood-like three-spoke rim blow steering wheel, reflective dual tape stripe on rear of spoiler and quarter panel extension, reflective two-tone body side tape stripe, teak-toned instrument panel and cluster appliques, floor console, bright-trimmed floor pedals, electric clock, swing-out quarter windows, tinted glass rear window, and rocker panel molding.

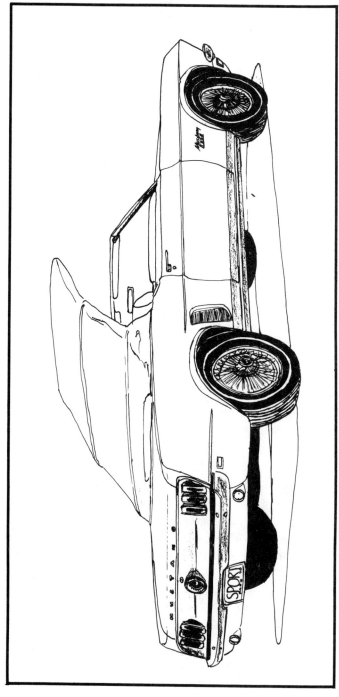

Convertible sales continued to fall and totalled less than 15,000 for the 1969 model year. The lowering mechanism was taken out of the fender wells in 1969, increasing rear seat room about ten inches.

BOSS 302 & 429, ROAD RACING & DRAGS

The Boss 302, offered at mid-year for $3,720, and the very limited production Boss 429, are sub-models of the sportsroof body style. The Boss 302 is a factory-built road racer which Ford designed to qualify for Trans-American sedan racing and to compete with the previously-introduced Chevrolet Camaro Z-28. Curiously, the Z-28 used a 302-cubic-inch engine with a 290 horsepower rating—the same figures as the Boss.

Similarly, the Boss 429 is a factory-made drag racer. The heavy engine up front did not help handling characteristics of the 429-engined car, while the 302 Boss used a very favorable power-to-weight ratio.

Standard equipment on the Boss 302, in addition to the engine included a four-speed, wide-ratio transmission (although some had the close-ratio because of availability problems), Hurst shifter, black taillamp bezels, black chrome backlite molding and black headlamp castings, color-keyed dual racing mirrors, black hood and rear deck lid and black lower back panel, F60-15 black sidewall tires with white lettering, dual exhausts, hub caps with trim rings, space saver spare, black tape indentification on front fender, quick-ratio steering (16:1), competition suspension, staggered rear shocks, front spoiler, power front disc brakes, 45 ampere battery, and 3.50 non-locking axle.

The Boss configuration with the special 429 CID racing-developed engine included a high-capacity engine oil cooler, 65 ampere alternator, 85 ampere battery mounted in the trunk, power steering with oil cooler, four-speed close ratio gearbox, power front disc brakes/rear drum brakes, "traction-lok" rear axle with 3.91 ratio standard, special high-performance suspension, front spoiler, F60 × 15 Super Wide Oval Fiberglass Belted Tires, "Magnum 500" 15 × 7-inch chrome-plated wheels, tachometer, interior decor group, console, high-back bucket seats with "comfortweave" vinyl, dual racing mirrors, visibility group, and deluxe seat belts.

TEN ENGINES INCLUDING TWO SIXES

For 1969, Ford produced ten basic engines for the Mustang. In the six-cylinder line, an improved placement of the engine mounts, four to six inches forward, alleviated much of the familiar vibration

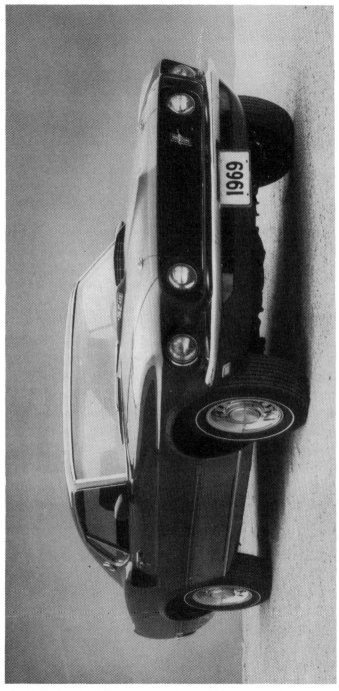

The new Mach I sportsroof sent production figures soaring for the fastback body style. This Mach I has the 428 Cobra Jet engine with ram air and qualifies as one of the top muscle cars of its day.

associated with the sixes. Engineers called this improvement "center percussion" mounting.

Although the durable 200 CID six again remained the basic engine, it was backed by a new optional six, the 250. For the first time since 1964, the Mustang used two different sixes. The 250 supplies 155 horsepower at 4,000 rpm and is essentially a 200 with a longer stroke. Bore and stroke equals 3.680 × 3.130 inches for the 200, and 3.682 × 3.910 inches for the larger 250. Each engine mounts the single Ford one-barrel carburetor with the intake manifold cast as an integral part of the cylinder head. Both engines were available with either the three-speed manual or the three Select Shift Cruise-O-Matic transmissions. Rear axle ratios varied between 2.79 and 3.08.

Ford sold the 302 in a tame two-barrel version and a high performance "Boss" form for 1969. The single two-barrel engine filled the slot vacated by the famous 289-2V. Bore and stroke were 4.00 × 3.00 inches, and the 302 produced 220 horsepower with a 9.5:1 compression using regular fuel.

Ford thought a lot of the Boss 302 performer, enough to name a car after it. The 302 is an impressive piece of machinery and represents the height of performance engineering with respect to the small block engine in the first generation Mustang. Newly-designed cylinder heads give the high-revving 302 its main advantage over the basic 302-2V. Valves are canted rather than straight to allow for larger intake and exhaust valves plus larger cylinder head ports that combine to give a straighter flow of gas in and out of the cylinders.

The combustion chambers, with their similarity to those of the racing 427, utilize an advanced wedge design for high turbulence. Other performance aspects include a mechanical camshaft, a forged steel crankshaft, forged steel connecting rods, pop-up pistons, ignition with dual point distributor, high-rise aluminum manifold with a monstrous 780 cfm carburetor, and an oil pan with a "windage baffle."

The crankshaft is balanced both statically and dynamically and held in place by five main bearings with the center three utilizing four bolts instead of the usual two. This engine was factory-rated at 290 horsepower at 5,800 rpm.

The four-speed transmission is the one method of transferring power to the rear axle for 1969. Like other V-8-engined cars, the

The ultimate streetable Mustang super car and perhaps the most highly desired muscle car Ford ever built, the famed Boss 302.

differential is of the straddle-mounted pinion type, but has the 31-spline shaft rather than the 28. Around 2,000 of the Boss 302 engines were produced in the latter half of 1969 with increased production in store for 1970 as word got around, and the engine became more available.

THE WILDEST BOSS YET

The new 429 CID engine replaced the extinct 427 in the Ford lineup and was offered in Boss form in the Mustang from the latter half of 1969 through 1970. The 429 is too big to fit a stock Mustang without cutting and fabricating which requires revising the spring towers and shock absorber mounts. This engine is easily identifiable by the small 14 mm spark plugs resting in slots on top of the heads! Other features of this engine include high-riser intake manifold, 735 CFM Holley four-barrel carburetor, dual point ignition, four-bolt main bearings, mechanical camming, and a host of other exotic engineering.

This wild engine does not make for good street driving, however, even to the man who wants a high-performance stormer. The cost was over $5,000, and Ford offered the car to the public for one main reason—to make it legal for stock car racing. Traction lok is standard with this Boss in a 3.91:1 ratio with 3.50's and the low, low 4.30's optional.

NEW 352 WINDSOR WAS FAVORITE

New for 1969 was the 351 cubic inch engine referred to as the 351 Windsor. Starting in 1969, the Windsor appeared in either two or four-barrel form. The 351, standard in Mach I's, weighed but 60 pounds more than the 302 and became a favorite of many buyers because it was a compromise between the small block 302's and the large block 390's, 428's, and 429's. Ford said the engine was "precision cast in the same manner as strong lightweight racing engines." In two-barrel form with 9.5:1 compression of the fuel/air mixture, the 351 had a peak horsepower rating of 250 at 4,400 rpm. The four barrel yielded 290 horses at 4,800 rpm with 10.7:1 compression that required premium fuel. All four transmissions mated to the all-purpose 351's, from the three-speed manual to the Select Shift automatic to the close or wide ratio four speed. Rear axle ratios varied from the 2.75's through the moderate 3.25's.

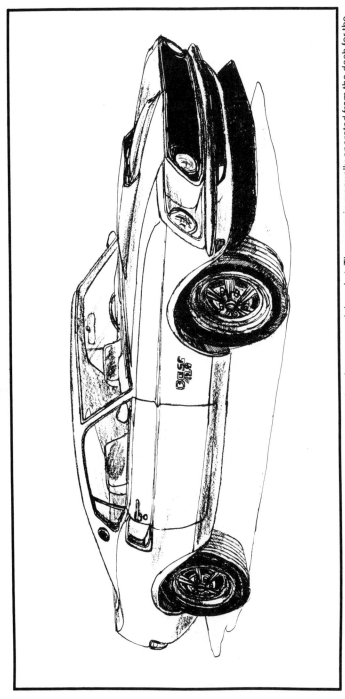

The limited production Boss 429 muscle car satisfied the appetite of a very special market. The scoop is manually operated from the dash for the ram air effect.

The 390 block appeared for the last time in a Mustang in 1969. With the changing, innovative engine lineup of the late Sixties, the 390 performer was pretty much obsolete by this year. Offered in four-barrel form only, it produced 320 horsepower at 4,600 rpm and required premium gasoline with the 10.5:1 pistons. The three-speed manual was the only transmission not seen mated to the big 390. Rear axle ratios ranged from the high-speed 2.75 through the lowest speed 4.30, revealing the flexibility of the 390.

428 COBRA JET & SUPER COBRA JET

After a mid-year start in 1968, the 428 street stormer returned as the Cobra Jet and a slightly new configurated Super Cobra Jet. Differences between the two are not super, however, but subtle. First, Super Cobra Jets came in cars equipped with the 3.90 or 4.30 rear axle. Super CJ's use the capscrew connecting rods rather than those with the nut and bolt; and SCJ's are distinguished by an oil cooler mounted in front of the radiator. Modified intake valve size is also slightly larger—2.097 inches versus the 2.092 inches of the standard CJ. The Select Shift Cruise-O-Matic and four-speed close ratio transmissions were the only available accompanying power teams with rear axle ratios varying from 3.25 to 4.30, with the 3.50's as standard. The 428's were available with or without the ram air via the functional shaker hood scoop.

SUDDEN GROWTH, LENGTH & WEIGHT

In 1969, Mustangs received completely new sheet metal in a longer, wider body. Although in four model years, Ford had added but two inches in overall length to their Mustang, the '69's at 187.4 inches are 3.8 inches longer than last year's offerings and 5.8 inches longer than the original pony. Since wheelbase remained the constant 108 inches, the length increases resulted from overhang. The width of 71.3 inches represents about a half-inch increase from last year, while each body style gained about 75 pounds. Approximate weights of the hardtop, sportsroof, and convertible with six-cylinder engines equals 2,832, 2,856, and 2,942 pounds, respectively. Mustang took advantage of a 20-gallon fuel tank this year.

SHEET METAL CHANGES

The second major restyling of the Mustang produced a car with very pleasing lines and that unmistakable Mustang look highly desired in 1969. The car displayed a bold performance look and stance especially in Mach I, sportsroof, or Boss configuration. The grilles in the 1969's are minus the familiar-framed Mustang emblem floating in the center of the grille face.

With styling reminiscent of the Shelbys, the front grille with black background mounts inboard driving lights at each end with a small, discrete Mustang emblem offset to the driver's side of the grille. To either side of the grille mouth are the other two headlamps positioned in sockets in the front fenders.

The hood could take several looks, and the weirdest resulted from the use of the "shaker" hood scoop for ram air. With the scoop mounted directly atop the motor and pushing through a hole cutout in the hood, it vibrated with the movement of the engine.

The other conventional hood was either functional for fresh cool air to the carburetor or non-functional for a simulated performance look.

Side sculpturing is less pronounced than ever, not missed perhaps because of the increased use of side striping. Mach I's, for example, used reflective dual tape stripes and identification that reminded one of the Shelby. The characteristic side scoop was raised a bit on the rear quarter panel of the fastbacks, positioned just behind the door handles. The Boss fastbacks, however, use no side scoop. On the convertible, hardtop, and Grande, the side scoop looked like a reversed scoop of years past with three groups of wind vanes for show.

REAR STYLING AND SPOILERS
A rearview of a 1969 Mustang reveals the triple lens taillight scheme and center-mounted gas cap embedded in the panel just above the rear bumper. The panel below the rear bumper does not use bumper guards this year, but mounts the standard backup lights in bright metal housings at each end of the panel.

The rear deck lid integrates a spoiler on the Mach I and sportsroof. The Boss uses an optional rear spoiler wing that is adjustable to improve rear-end stability and a sportslats option that keeps rain and direct sunlight off the backlite glass.

Other option/accessories altering the exterior begin with the exterior decor group that included bright wheel opening moldings,

The interior look of the Mustang changed more than ever this year as revealed by the inside of this Grande. Interiors displayed a sports car look, but used luxury as a major selling point.

rear deck moldings on hardtop and convertible, full wheel covers, and rocker panel molding.

The GT Equipment Group for V-8 cars consists of dual exhausts and quad outlets (except with the 302-2V), wide oval-belted tires, styled steel wheels, stiffer shocks, heavy-duty springs, and larger diameter stabilizer bar, pop-open gas cap, pin-type hood lock latches, stripes and functional hood air scope with the Cobra Jet ram air, and GT ornamentation.

Other exterior-featured options include the power convertible top, two-tone hood, vinyl roof on hardtop in black or parchment, remote control left-hand outside mirror, convertible glass backlite, front bumper guards, and tinted glass. Convertibles used a better designed top linkage in 1969 in which the lowering mechanism was taken out of the rear quarter panels; rear-seat room is increased about ten inches as a result.

INTERIOR, FANCY AND COMFORTABLE

On the inside the '69 Mustang displays a richer and more luxurious look than past years, but also is very sporty. The optional

106

A 1969 Shelby GT-500 convertible. Shelby's received their first total restyling in 1969 although they were entering their last full year of production.

high-backed bucket seats provide one of the most comfortable seats of any car in the country in 1969. The dual cockpit-style padded dash is impressive, especially with the teak-toned instrument panel utilizing a full set of circular working gauges in front of the driver and an electric clock with sweep-second hand for the front seat passenger. Although the glove box in the dash is very small, an optional safety padded console gives extra room with a built-in compartment between the bucket seats. The full bench seat was also buyable this year to try and satisfy special Mustang riders—a feature not found in other ponycars.

Steering wheels are of the three-spoked variety; heating and air conditioning controls are centrally located for driver and passenger use; front leg room increases with more free travel rearward in the individually-adjustable bucket seats. Still, an interior decor group would make a deluxe car out of hardtop, convertible, or sportsroof. It included deluxe seat trim with comfortweave vinyl inserts, safety/courtesy door lights, molded door trim panels with integral arm rests, deluxe three-spoke wood-toned rim blow steering wheel, and remote control left-hand outside mirror.

The deluxe interior decor group (convertible and sportsroof only) added a teak-toned instrument panel and cluster appliques, and an electric clock. The visibility group this year included a remote control outside left-hand mirror, light and lock for glove box, ash tray light, luggage compartment light, an under dash light in the hardtop, parking brake warning light, and a lighted ignition switch.

Other factory-interior-appointed option/accessories of popularity are the AM/FM stereo radio, stereosonic tape/AM radio system, SelectAire Conditioner, console, front bench seat, comfortweave vinyl seat upholstery, high-backed bucket seats, deluxe seat belts and shoulder belts (except convertibles), fingertip speed control (with V-8 and Select Shift), tachometer (with V-8's), folding rear seat for sportsroof and Mach I, and intermittent windshield wipers. An optional power ventilation system supplemented the standard heating and ventilating system.

CHANGES IN SUSPENSIONS AND SHELBYS

Changes to improve the suspension of 1969 Mustangs were a result of the needs of the production factory super cars—the Boss

302, Boss 429, and 428 CJ's. These cars use a competition suspension option similar to the one abandoned in 1967, but with staggered rear shocks. By placing the right shock ahead of the axle and the left shock behind the axle, vibration associated with the live rear axle in the left spring setup is damped out substantially. The Bosses also added a rear stabilizer bar which would be added next year to the competition suspension package. Overall manual steering ratios remained 25.3:1 and with power assist, 20.3:1 with a turning diameter of 37.6 feet.

The Shelby Mustangs received their first total major restyling in 1969, but for less than obvious reasons. Increased performance cars like the Mach I's and Bosses helped end production of the Shelbys. Production remained a low 3,150 with the total broken down into the following:

GT-350	Fastback	1,085
	Convertible	194

GT-500	Fastback	1,536
	Convertible	335

Although the GT-350 lists a 302, research shows none were built with this engine. The ram air 351 was the choice for the GT-350, while the GT-500 used a ram air 428.

1970:
Still No. 1 but Fading

Mustang entered the 1970 new-car market with body style designations similar to 1969, but again incorporating new design features and styling changes to help keep it the number one seller in the sporty, speciality car field. Production figures, however, dropped over 100,000 units from the previous model year.

Meanwhile, Ford's under $2,000 Maverick, although offered in the single two-door sedan body style and still minus a V-8 engine option, sold a fantastic 451,081 cars in its first full model year. Sales of the ponycars, however, had been dropping for the last few years and no longer garnered the 10% share of total industry sales they once enjoyed. But Mustang captured first place in sales in its field for the model year, accounting for 190,727 units compared to 124,899 for the closest competitor, the Chevrolet Camaro. The Mustang lineup with respect to body number is as follows:

Body	
#63A	Two-Door Fastback—Standard
#63B	Two-Door Fastback—Deluxe
#63C	Two-Door Fastback—Mach I
#65A	Two-Door Hardtop—Standard
#65B	Two-Door Hardtop—Deluxe
#65E	Two-Door Hardtop—Grande
#76A	Convertible—Standard
#76B	Convertible—Deluxe

Body Numbers 65C and 65D are missing from the 1970 lineup—the standard and deluxe bench seat models. Although a buyer could order a bench seat, these cars were no longer distinguished by body numbers. Mach I sales cooled off to 40,970, while the standard fastback lacked exactly 1,500 units of equalling that figure. Convertible sales dropped under 10,000 for the first time, while the hardtop remained the most popular, but failed to reach 100,000 units. The Boss 302 and Boss 429 returned after a mid-year introduction in 1969, and utilized the sportsroof body.

RUNDOWN OF THE STANDARD HARDTOP

The hardtop sold for $2,721 this year with the following standard features: 200 CID "Big Six;" fully-synchronized three-speed manual transmission; floor-mounted shift lever; color-keyed loop pile carpeting; courtesy lights; cigarette lighter; reversible keys; keyless locking; heater/defroster; all-vinyl interior; curved side glass; high-back bucket seats; locking steering column; twice-a-year maintenance; glove box; color-keyed headlining; printed circuit instrument panel; aluminized and stainless steel muffler; E78 × 14 belted bias ply tires; and the Ford Motor Company Lifeguard Safety Features. New safety features for 1970 included a non-reversing odometer, parking lamps coupled with the headlamps, and a safety glove box latch. Also, 1970 Fords use the three-way locking steering column with the ignition key located in the steering column.

GRANDE AND CONVERTIBLE FEATURES

The Mustang Grande retailed for $2,926, just $205 more than the hardtop with the following additional features; a special sound insulating package; luxury cloth and vinyl seat trim; molded door trim panels and courtesy lights; deluxe two-spoke steering wheel; woodtone instrument panel appliques; electric clock; bright floor pedal trim; dual color-keyed racing mirrors that included a remote control left-hand mirror; dual body side paint stripe; black or white "Landau" vinyl roof covering; houndstooth-check interior trim fabrics in five colors; and glove compartment lock.

For $3,025, the convertible offered the same standard features of the hardtop plus the following: a five-ply power-operated vinyl top; glass backlite; color-keyed boot; easy-action top fastening

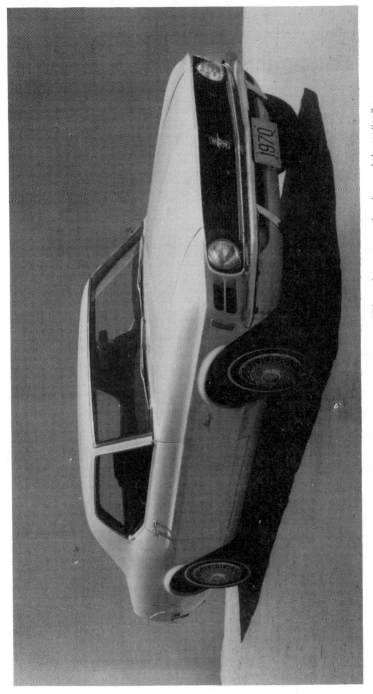

The basic hardtop. Ford sold less than 100,000 of these for the first time in 1970, and ponycar sales dropped dramatically.

latches; full-width rear seat; and courtesy lights under the instrument panel.

Likewise, the sportsroof gave the buyer, for $2,771, the extra features of an integral rear deck spoiler, swing-out rear quarter windows, tinted glass backlite, and courtesy lights under the instrument panel and rear compartment. For another $500, the sportsroof became a Mach I with a long list of extras: 351-2V engine; non-functional hood scoop/integral turn signal indicators; competition suspension; outside color-keyed dual racing mirrors; knitted vinyl high-back bucket seats; console with woodtone applique; rim-blow deluxe three-spoke steering wheel; bright dual exhaust extensions; hood lock pins; honeycomb back panel applique; wide oval-belted WSW tires; pop-open gas cap; dark argent extruded aluminim rocker panel molding; deck lid tape stripe (diecast "Mach I"); black painted hood and tape engine numerals (white painted hood and tape engine numerals available with black or dark green); die-cast center deep dish sports wheel covers; sport lamps in grille; woodtone cluster with right-hand instrument panel applique; electric clock; bright pedal pads; molded door trim panels with courtesy lights; NVH sound package; and carpet runners.

BOSS 302 AND BOSS 429 CONTINUED

The price of the Boss 302, $3,720, included the standard equipment of the hardtop and the sportsroof plus the following: 302-4V V-8 engine rated at 290 horsepower; four-speed manual transmission with Hurst Shifter; black taillamp bezels; black chrome backlite molding and black headlamp castings; color-keyed dual racing mirrors; black hood and rear deck lid and black lower back panel; F60-15 belted BSW tires with white letters; hub cap/trim ring; space-saver spare; bodyside/hood stripes; Boss 302 tape identification on front fender (black only); dual exhausts; quick ratio steering (16:1); competition suspension; special cooling package; 3.50 non-locking axle; front spoiler; 45-ampere battery; and power front disc brakes.

The Boss 429, a member of the sports-roof body style, returned in 1970 in similar form to the one introduced in mid-1969. Of course, the Mustang engine compartment still could not hold the big 429 without cutting and fabricating, and the Boss 429 remained a limited production car with a very special market.

The 1970 Mach I with 428 CJR and shaker hood scoop. Mach I sales cooled off this year although it continued to display a bold performance look similar to 1969.

TWO SIXES AND FIVE V-8S

Two six-cylinders were available for 1970—the 200 and the 250. Ford called the 200 the "Big Six" this year because for the first time it used improved heads with larger ports and valves interchangeable with the head/intake manifold of the larger 250, but with a combustion chamber accommodating the lower compression of the 200. The 200 rated 120 horsepower at 4,400 rpm with the 8.7:1 compression ratio and single Ford one-barrel carburetor.

The 250, recommended for use with power options like air conditioning, provided 155 horsepower at 4,400 rpm with 9.0:1 compression and single one-barrel Carter carburetor. Either the three-speed manual or the Cruise-O-Matic transmissions were mated to the sixes, with 2.79, 2.83, 3.00, or 3.08 rear axle ratios.

The V-8 engines for 1970 begin with the popular 302-2V. With the Autolite two-barrel carburetor, it rated 210 horsepower at 4,400 rpm. With the 9.5:1 compression and burning regular fuel, this engine is the same one introduced in 1969 models.

Its high-performance counterpart, the 302 Boss performer, introduced in the 1969-½-model year, was offered a second year with some design changes. Most notable changes included the reduction of the intake valves from a massive 2.23 inches to 2.19 inches for greater clearance with the exhaust valve. (With the canted valve design, the intake and exhaust valves could actually cross paths at high rpm.) 1970 Boss engines, which were also sold this year in Mercury Cougars, contained an electronic rev limiter. This device cuts the electrical impulse to spark plugs randomly to maintain less than 6,150 rpm (±20). The limiter began working at around 5,800 rpm, but with recommended shift points in all gears at 5,700 rpm, the engine is quite effective. Of course, the high-revving 302 can easily be wound to seven grand by replacing the limiter with regular coil circuitry.

With the single four-barrel Holley carburetor, 10.5:1 compression ratio, high-rise aluminum manifold, solid valve lifters, dual exhausts, and more, this engine is rated a conservative 290 horsepower at 5,800 rpm with potential for much improvement to the enthusiast.

FOUR-SPEED WITH TWO RATIOS

The four-speed manual with standard Hurst shifter was the one transmission available with the Boss, but in either wide or close

116

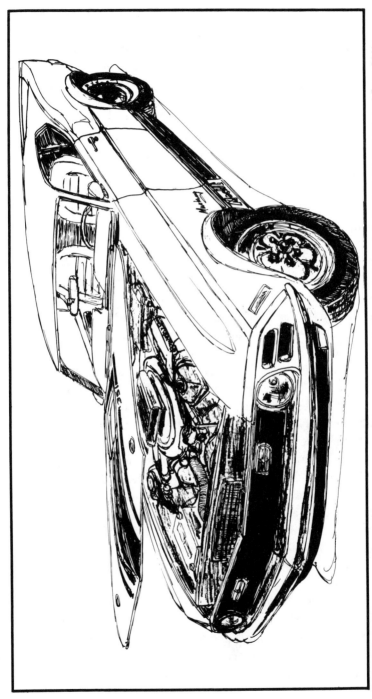

The shaker hood scoop, introduced in 1969, was in use for one last year, but expanded to include the 351-2V, 351-4V, and Boss 302's.

ratio. The close-ratio uses a low-gear ratio of 2.32, second gear ratio of 1.69, third gear ratio of 1.29, and the 1.00 ratio for fourth. The wide-ratio uses a low-gear ratio of 2.78, a second gear ratio of 1.93, a third gear ratio of 1.36, and a fourth gear ratio of 1.00. The later (wide-ratio) is most favorable in the Boss 302 as the torque advantage of the lower speed helps the engine in the lower rpm range where it is most needed. The big block, low rpm, high-torque engines are more suited to the higher speed (closer) gear ratios. Third member rear axle ratios varied from the standard 3.50 non-locking to the traction lok 3.50, 3.91, and new Detroit Automotive No-Spin 4.30. This "No-Spin" differential is a competition-proved setup that provides maximum traction by dividing the torque equally to both wheels.

DIFFERING WINDSOR AND CLEVELAND 351S

The 351 cubic inch V-8, introduced in 1969 in the Mustang, powered Mustangs with either the 351 "Windsor" or the newly-engineered 351 "Cleveland." The Windsor used a two-barrel carburetor while the Cleveland appeared with either two or four barrel, and is different from the Windsor in important respects.

The Cleveland takes advantage of the canted valve head design which allows for bigger valves in better designed ports for increased flow of the fuel/air mixture through the engine. Intake valves measure 2.19 inches with 1.71-inch exhaust valves on the Cleveland four barrel—the same size as used on the 1970 Boss 302. The Cleveland heads with the two-barrel have slightly smaller ports and valves.

The new block casting of the 351 Clevelands extends forward to integrate the timing chain chamber, water cross-over passage, heater supply outlet, and water bypass opening. The water cross-over passage frees the intake manifold on the Cleveland from handling water flow from one side of the V-8 engine to the other, allowing for better shaping of the intake manifold and improved flow of the air/gas mix.

The two-barrel, in Windsor or Cleveland form, rates 250 horsepower at 4,600 rpm with a 9.5:1 compression ratio and burns regular fuel. The four-barrel Cleveland, with a very high 11.4:1 compression ratio is rated a peak 300 horsepower at 5,400 rpm. Each of the 351's uses hydraulic valve lifters and strong forged steel

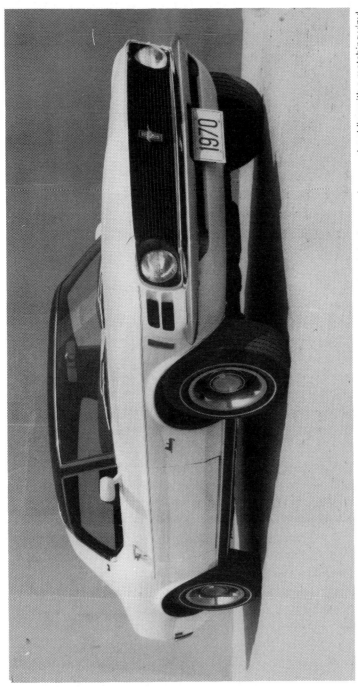

The 1970 Mustang Grandes are very sharp-looking cars with the three-quarter vinyl roof and aluminum rocker panel molding with a matching vinyl insert.

connecting rods, while main bearing diameter is 2.75 inches for the Cleveland and 3.00 inches for the Windsor.

Spark plugs for the Cleveland are much smaller than on the Windsor and fit a 14mm hole, while the Windsor plugs fit a 18mm spark plug hole. Each of the 351 CID engines (the 302 also), with power steering or air conditioning, uses a new dual accessory belt setup that drives the water pump separately from the alternator. Higher alternator output and longer life for the water pump and belts are an advantage of this setup.

LAST TIME FOR THE COBRA JETS

The big 428 Cobra Jet made its last showing in a Mustang in 1970. Called the base muscle engine by Ford, the 428 again rated the very conservative 335 horsepower at 5,200 rpm with a 10.6:1 compression ratio.

A 428 became a 428 Super Cobra Jet with the optional Drag Pack features—traction-lok differential with 3.91 axle ratio or "Detroit Locker" no-spin differential with 4.30 axle ratio, plus engine modifications that included use of an engine oil cooler, cap-screw connecting rods, modified crankshaft, modified flywheel, and modified vibration damper. Select Shift Cruise-O-Matic and close ratio four-speed manual were available with the 428. With the many possible applications of the 428, a wide range of axle ratios applied for 1970, including the 3.00, 3.25, 3.50, 3.91, and 4.30.

SLIGHT STYLING CHANGES

After a major reshaping in 1969, exteriors of the 1970 models include design differences that allow one to distinguish it from the earlier Mustang. Beginning with the front end, the most obvious change is the return to single headlights. The grille is made up of horizontal black bars with the small Mustang emblem embedded in its center. To either side of the headlights the fender extensions incorporate simulated air scoops. The Mach I differs slightly with integral sport lamps in its blackout-type grille which does not use a Mustang emblem. The Boss models use the Mustang emblem, but mount it offset to the driver's side.

Bright metal front bumper guards were optional this year mounted vertical to the panel below the front bumper. The parking

The sportsroof with unique side striping and hub caps/trim rings, sometimes called "deep dish" wheels. The slots adjacent to the headlights in the fender extensions are simulated air scoops.

121

lights/turn signals at the ends of the horizontal opening below the front bumper flash alternately with the side marker lights for the first time this year. 1970 Mustangs also have for the first time access holes in the headlight trim for external adjustment of the beams; it is no longer necessary to remove the headlight bezel to get at the adjusting screws.

With respect to the hood, the "shaker" scoop was still in use for one last year and expanded to the 351-2V, 351-4V, and Boss 302 engines in addition to the 428 CJ-R. The Boss 302 used a black striping of the hood, as did the Mach I with black or green stripe and engine numerals identifying the engine size.

Mach I models also contained a new, very wide aluminum rocker panel molding located between the front and rear wheelwells with large Mach I letters. The Grande mounted a narrower aluminum rocker panel molding with a vinyl applique.

Another body side feature of the 1970 Grandes is a dual paint stripe wrapping around the front fender extension and running to the rear quarter panel. Grandes also contain a black or white three-quarter vinyl roof in the style of the Thunderbird Landau of 1970.

Design of the rear end changed little from 1969, but new recessed taillamps/turn signals also blink alternately with the side marker lights which are located in the sheet metal of the rear quarter panel.

Rear quarter panel sheet metal is newly designed in the hardtop. The rear-mounted adjustable spoiler and backlite louvers seen on the Boss 302 last year were extended this year to the sportsroof models. A new "houndstooth" vinyl roof covering for hardtops in two basic colors (blue or green) complemented the body color. It also complemented or matched the new houndstooth upholstery in the Grande hardtop. Mach I's use a new "honeycomb" back panel applique with die cast Mach I capital letters centered in the deck lid. A power top is standard on the Mustang for the first time this year.

HIGH-BACK SEATS LEAD INTERIOR FEATURES

On the interior, Mustangs use the comfortable high-back bucket seats as standard equipment, which eliminates the need for the padded head restraints. Front seat back latches are standard again this year, but a new convenience group option contained an automatic seat back release. Triggered by a plunger-type switch in the "A" pillar, it releases both front seat latches when either door is opened. Other features of the convenience panel are trunk light, glove compartment light, left-hand remote control mirror, parking brake warning light, and courtesy lights under the instrument panel (on the hardtops and sportsroofs).

Deluxe cars use the decor group, which consists of knitted vinyl or blazer stripe cloth and vinyl trim with high-back bucket seats, woodtone instrument panel appliques, deluxe two-spoke steering wheel, color-keyed racing mirrors with remote control on left-hand mirror, rocker panel and wheel lip moldings, and formed door trim panels (with courtesy lights on the convertible).

The tilt steering wheel in 1970 has five driving positions. The two- or three-spoked steering wheels are of a new oval design in which the upper half is molded in a 15½-inch round diameter and the lower half is formed of a 14½-inch diameter oval. A new rim blowing method is used this year in which pressure exerted anywhere around the surface of the spokes causes the horn to blow.

The four-pod instrument cluster in front of the driver consists of a fuel gauge, speedometer/odometer, tachometer, and water temperature gauge, with the oil pressure and alternator indicators in warning lights. Transmissions use the floor-mounted shift lever, as always, and four-speed manuals use the Hurst shifters with a "T" handle grip. Steering columns use the anti-theft locking system for the first time in 1970.

Mustangs also use a new pressure relief ventilation system in which air outlet openings beneath the rear seat allow air to enter the trunk compartment and travel through the inner body panels to a pressure relief valve in the door lock pillar.

FLAIR GROUP OF OPTIONS NEW

A new optional flair group extended the availability of the new high-back decor bucket seats, standard in the Grande and Mach I, to all model Mustangs. The flair group also included a choice of knitted vinyl or cloth and vinyl upholstery (convertibles use the knitted vinyl only), plus woodtone instrument panel appliques, a deluxe two-spoke steering wheel, color-keyed dual racing mirrors, rocker panel moldings, and wheel lip moldings.

Other interior-appointed factory-installed option/accessories of interest include a rectangular electric clock, a circular electric clock (like seen on the Grande and Mach I), console, rear window defogger, deluxe seat belts with reminder light, intermittent windshield wipers, color-keyed dual racing mirrors (like seen on the Grande, Mach I, and those cars with the Flair Group), rear seat sport deck option (sportsroof only), and complete tinted glass.

IMPORTANT SUSPENSION IMPROVEMENTS

Suspension and resulting handling improved in 1970. A rear stabilizer added to the Mach I and the competition suspension option combined with the stiffer springs and shocks, larger diameter front stabilizer bar, and staggered rear shock absorbers to create a car of near competition status. The quick ratio steering (16:1), was offered this year without the power assist. Generally, the lighter sixes exhibit oversteer, the medium weight 302's and 351's have about neutral steering characteristics, while the heavy 400 plus cubic inch engine cars understeer somewhat.

Rear axle ratios of 3.50, 3.91, or 4.30 use an extra strength cast nodular iron center section, a larger axle shaft with 31 splines compared to the 28 splines in other ratios, and fully-machined axle shafts to help prevent build-up of stress points.

Basic manual steering ratios equal 25.4:1, and the basic power-assisted steering ratio equals 20.5:1. E70 × 14 belted WSW tires were standard with wide oval E70 and F70 belted WSW tires and F60 × 15's with raised white letters on the Boss 302.

DIMENSIONS OF THE '70'S & THE LAST OF THE SHELBYS

With respect to dimensions and capacities, the 1970 Mustangs remained the same length as last year (187.4"), added .4" in width (from 71.3" to 71.7"), remained about the same height at slightly over 51", and used the same tread widths of 58.5" front and rear. With the small trunk area, the space saver (collapsable) spare tire is almost a necessity for better luggage and carrying capacity. The fuel tank again was increased in size from 20 to 22 gallons unless the car sold in California, in which case capacity remained 20 gallons. The Boss 429 gas tank also remained 20 gallons. Overall, 1970 Mustangs weigh about 200 pounds more than the 1969's. With six-cylinder

The super muscle car, the Boss 302, returned for its second and final year in 1970. The distinctive side striping gives away the high-performance engineering of the small block 302 nestled beneath its hood.

engines, the hardtop, sportsroof, and convertible weigh approximately 3,080, 3,104, and 3,190 pounds, respectively.

The Shelby models sold in 1970 for the last time. Production ceased in July of 1969; and 1970 Shelbys are really leftover 1969 models that were re-modified with front spoilers and new stripe identification. By the start of the 1970 model year, Ford was really into the performance scene with the Boss 302, Boss 429, and the popular Mach I.

1971:
Longer, Lower, Wider

The 1971 Mustang was the most changed model since Ford started production of the ponycar in 1964. It was longer, lower, and wider in a completely restyled body that Ford claimed reminded one of "the most expensive personal sports cars." European sports cars like Ferrari, Maserati, and Lamborghini come to mind as well as Ford's own Mark II and Mark IV racing cars.

The model offering included the hardtop, convertible, and sportsroof, again with Grande, Mach I, and a new "Boss," the Boss 351 sportsroof. Wheelbase increased for the first time in Mustang's history, from 108 to 109 inches.

Although the new Mustangs of 1971 are but a couple of inches longer overall than 1970, they look much bigger. The exterior and interior of the '71's sported new design features, while the wider stance gave the driver of the new Mustang a different feel of the road, especially on corners. Although the total number of engines dropped again this year, some new performers powered these highly-styled and luxurious Mustangs.

PRODUCTION AND BODY LINEUP

Although ponycar sales continued to slip, 149,678 Mustangs left assembly plants in Dearborn, Michigan, and Metuchen, New Jersey, while its closest competitor the Chevrolet Camaro totalled

114,643. Other ponycars included the Mercury Cougar (62,864), Pontiac Firebird (53,124), American Motors Javelin (26,866), and Plymouth Barracuda (18,690). The Mustang lineup for 1971 with respect to body number is as follows:

Body	
#63D	Two-Door Fastback—Standard
#63R	Two-Door Fastback—Mach I
#65D	Two-Door Hardtop—Standard
#65F	Two-Door Hardtop—Grande
#76D	Convertible—Standard

Of the basic hardtop, 65,696 of Body #65D sold with a base price of $2,911 with the following standard features: 250 CID "Big Six" engines; fully-synchronized three-speed manual transmission; concealed windshield wipers and cool air inlet; DirectAire Ventilation; floor-mounted shift lever; recessed exterior door handles; arm rests; color-keyed loop-pile carpeting; courtesy lights; cigarette lighter; reversible keys; keyless locking; heater/defroster; all-vinyl interior; curved side glass; high-back bucket seats; locking steering column; twice-a-year maintenance; glove box; color-keyed headlining; printed circuit instrument cluster; aluminized and stainless steel muffler components; E78-14 belted bias BSW tires; back panel applique; plus the Ford Lifeguard Design Safety Features seen in 1970.

GRANDE, CONVERTIBLE AND SPORTSROOF FEATURES

The Grande hardtop retailed for $3,117, and exactly 17,406 of these more luxurious hardtops were built in 1971 with the features of the hardtop plus the following: luxury cloth and vinyl seat trim; door trim panels with integral handles; arm rests; and courtesy lights; deluxe two-spoke steering wheel; black instrument panel appliques; electric clock; bright floor pedal trim; dual color-keyed racing mirrors with remote control LH mirror; dual bodyside paint stripe; vinyl roof covering; interior trim fabrics in five colors; wheel covers; rocker panel molding; wheel lip molding; and bright weatherstrip retainer.

Ford constructed a total of 6,121 convertibles this year with a base cost of $3,227 with the features of the hardtop plus the follow-

A 1971 Mustang Grande. The longer, lower, and wider '71's are the most changed Mustangs since the original, but appear much bigger than they really are.

ing: a five-ply power-operated vinyl top; glass backlite; color-keyed boot; easy-action top fastening latches; full-width rear seat; courtesy lights under instrument panel; and bright upper back panel molding.

For an extra $62, the sportsroof contained the features of the hardtop (with the exception of the back panel applique with bright molding), plus the tinted glass backlite and a rear tape strip.

Production of this basic fastback style, Body #63D, stood at a low 23,596 at the end of the 1971 model year. The higher-priced Mach I sportsroof, however, sold about one and a half times that amount. This higher production is understandable when one looks at the extra standard equipment of the Mach I delivered for a $295 increase in price: 302-2V V-8 engine; choice of hood with or without NASA-type hood scoops; E70-14 wide oval WSW tires; color-keyed spoiler bumper; honeycomb texture grille; competition suspension; dual color-keyed racing mirrors with remote control LH mirror; dual exhausts; honeycomb black panel applique; pop-open gas cap; wheel trim rings/hub caps; sport lamps in grille; Mach I fender decals; black or argent lower body; front and rear valance panels; and rear tape stripe with Mach I decal.

BOSS 351 IN THE SPORTSROOF

Also using the sportsroof body style, the high-performing Boss 351 retailed for $4,124 with the standard equipment of the hardtop and the sportsroof plus the following: 351-4V, V-8 engine rated at 330 horsepower; black or argent hood; four-speed manual transmission with Hurst shifter; color-keyed dual racing mirrors; black or argent lower back panel and lower bodyside; front and rear valance panels; F60-15 BSW tires with raised white letters; hub cap/trim rings; space saver spare tire; bodyside tape stripes; Boss 351 tape identification on front fenders and deck lid; dual exhausts; competition suspension including staggered rear shocks, special cooling package; 3.91 ratio traction-lok differential; electronic rpm limiter; tachometer; trip odometer; and oil temperature, ammeter, water temperature gauges; 80-ampere battery; power front disc brakes; and black front spoiler.

LAST PRODUCTION SUPER CAR

Transition best describes the 1971 model year with respect to engines. The abundance of high compression big cube engines re-

Bars returned to the front grille for the first time since 1967. This is the basic Mustang sportsroof, Body #63D. The fastback styling of the sportsroof is exaggerated to the extent that it is sometimes called a "flatback."

quiring premium fuel dwindled, and 1971 gave the consumer his last chance to buy a Mustang factory super car. Low lead gasolines were promoted in the push to lower exhaust emissions. Engine sizes ranges from the 250 six to the monstrous 429 Cobra Jet. The 250 CID six-cylinder with single, one-barrel Carter carburetor develops 145 horsepower at 4,000 rpm with a 9.0:1 compression ratio. This engine is the one six offered on 1971 Mustangs, as the smaller 200 was dropped from the Mustang lineup this year. Standard gears are the 3.00's with or without traction-lok if the three-speed manual was ordered. With the Cruise-O-Matic, these same gears were optional while the 2.79's were standard. The four-speed was not listed as available with the six.

The 302-2V and the 351-2V made up the economy V-8 engine list for 1971. The 302, a continuation from 1970, rated a maximum 210 horsepower at 4,600 rpm with 9.0:1 compression, while the 351 (Cleveland or Windsor) produced 240 horsepower at 4,600 rpm with 9.0:1 compression. Both engines, of course, use regular gasoline. Rear axle ratios included a 2.75 and a 2.79, standard on the 302 and 351 respectively, plus the optional 3.00 and 3.25 ratios that could be ordered with traction-lok. The four-speed manual was also not listed with these engines.

V-8'S INCLUDE LOW AND HIGH OUTPUT 351'S

The other engines appearing in 1971 Mustangs came with four-barrel carburetors. The Mustang sales brochure lists the 351-4V, the 351-HO Boss, the 429 CJ, and 429 CJ-R, the R denoting ram air. The 351-4V Cleveland returned this year with a slightly lower compression ratio of 10.7:1—still quite high, however, and requiring premium fuel. With the stock Autolite carburetor, this engine produced 285 horsepower at 5,400 rpm. Later in the 1971 model year, however, Ford added a low-compression-performance-type 351 Cleveland to the lineup that was called the 351 CJ. Its improved performance features included a high lift and longer duration cam, rugged four-bolt main bearing caps, 750 CFM carburetor, special intake manifold, higher pressure valve springs, larger inertia member vibration damper, special header-type exhaust manifolds, and a dual exhaust system. It rated 280 horsepower at 5,800 rpm and burned regular fuel with a 9.0:1 compression ratio. Mated to the

The 1971 Mach I. Some of these cars are powered by the 429 Cobra Jet and could combine features like air conditioning and power steering with the "digger"-type 3.91 rear axle ratio.

133

four-speed wide ratio transmission, or the Cruise-O-Matic, gear ratios for the 351's included the 3.00, 325, or 3.50 with or without traction-lok.

Ford replaced the Boss 302 in 1971 with a new "Boss," the 351-4V-HO (high output). Specially prepared by Holman & Moody, noted race car engine builders, the 351-4V rated a factory conservative 330 horsepower with high performance and durability features such as the following: four-bolt main caps; special high-tensile strength rod cap bolts and nuts; forged steel rods (shot peened and magnafluxed); heads with screw in rocker studs; high-strength forged aluminum pop-up pistons; a phosphate-coated, hardened cast iron camshaft for mechanical lifters; high output oil pump; stiff valve springs; and a cast iron big port manifold mounting the new 750 CFM Autolite four-barrel. Heads are of the regular 351-4V with large ports and valves—2.19″ for intale and 1.71″ for exhaust—that are canted in two planes.

The Boss 351, however, never reached the popularity of the first Boss; but it was sold for only one year and did not have much of a chance to catch on. Electronic rpm limiters are standard on the new Boss, designed to protect the engine from over-revving. But the longer stroke of the 351 (3.5″ vs. 3.0″ in the Boss 302) decreases the revving ability of this engine. And the crankshaft of the 351, although specially selected of cast nodular iron for durability and strengh, is not as strong or durable as the forged steel crank in the Boss 302, and not as able to stand higher range rpm's, like above 7,000.

LAST YEAR FOR THE 429 COBRA JET

Ford offered the big 429 Cobra Jets in Mustangs on a regular production basis for the first time in 1971; but ironically, also for the last time this year. Ford built the engine for the hardtop, sportsroof, convertible, Mach I, and even the luxury-appointed Grande. The increased size of the engine compartment with the widened front track and revised front-end geometry allowed the 429 to fit these cars without cutting and fabricating.

The 429 CJ became a 429 SCJ with the "Drag Pack" option that include the standard Mach I NASA-type hood, long duration, high-lift cam with mechanical lifters, cap screw connecting rods, modified crank-shaft, modified flywheel, modified vibration damper, and a locking differential with 3.91:1 traction-lok or 4.11:1 Detroit Locker no-spin ratio.

The Super Cobra Jet also has an engine oil cooler mounted on the side of the engine, a higher capacity oil pump, and a larger flow carburetor—780 CFM, plus four-bolt mains. So, whereas the Cobra Jet is an improved performance version of the stock 429 of the regular Ford lines (Thunderbird, for example), the Super Cobra Jet is an improved performance version of the Cobra Jet of the Ford muscle car lines. The SCJ is more suited to drag racing applications.

With respect to the 492 CJ, camming is hydraulic with stiff valve springs and 2.24″ intake valves, 1.72″ exhaust valves—the largest valves to date on a stock Mustang. Other features include a 750 CFM Autolite carburetor, beefed rods, special ignition, and special streamlined exhaust manifolds. The 429 CJ rated 370 horsepower at 5,600 rpm while the 429 SCJ rated a conservative five additional horsepower with its Drag Pack features. Transmission options included Select Shift and the close ratio, four-speed manual. So, again no transmission is standard, but one must be ordered at extra cost. Gear ratios for the CJ are the standard 3.50's or the optional 3.25's and 3.50's with traction-lok. A buyer could actually order a 429 SCJ with a traction-look 3.91 rear axle ratio and still have luxury features like air conditioning, power steering, and power disc brakes!

COMPLETE CHANGE IN APPEARANCE

From bumper to bumper, the 1971 Mustangs are set apart from any previous Mustang ever built. Beginning with the front-end arrangement, the hardtop, Grande, and sportsroof models employ a deeply-recessed plastic, argent (silver) colored grille encased by a right plated frame. This wide mount grille is divided by the large galloping Mustang emblem and flanking horizontal bars. Single head-lamps are contained in adjacent sheet metal housings painted in color of the body. Also, bright moldings around the leading edge of the hood and fenders enclose the grille and headlights.

The Mach I and Boss 351, however, have a slightly different look with a black honeycomb grille mounting sport lamps and a small center-positioned Mustang emblem. Sheet metal back-grounding the headlights is painted black rather than the body color.

Also, a new urethane bumper separated the Mach I and Boss 351 from the rest of the lineup. Color-keyed to the body and shaped somewhat like a blade, the new bumper "doubled as an efficient air spoiler" according to Ford. It can also take low speed bumps and retain its shape. The Boss 351's standard equipment also includes an air spoiler below the front bumper.

The sloped, elongated hood of the 1971 Mustang is contoured to conceal the windshield wipers and the cowl air inlets, giving it uninterrupted smooth lines. Optional hood scoops (functional or non-functional), are twin NASA-type, that blend with the shape of the hood. Ford made the hood scoop contours similar to scoops designed by NASA (National Aeronautics and Space Administration) for the latest jet aircraft. They are functional with cars with the ram air option and provide low levels for air turbulence and skin friction with maximum laminar air flow in a wide speed range.

SIDES AND ROOFLINES ALL DIFFERENT

The sides of Mustang bodies are distinguished this year by "flush" door handles with a recessed trip that pulls up and out to open the door, steel guard rails in the doors to help absorb side impact forces, and flaired wheel openings to accommodate wide tires. Hardtops have a design feature known as "tunnel backlite" in which the rear window is recessed between roof pillars that slope from the back of the roof to the rear deck.

The fastback styling of the sportsroof is exaggerated to the extent that it is sometimes called a "flatback." Its rear window is nearly parallel to the ground.

Each body style uses a thinner roof section than any previous model year car, and also employs thinner windshield pillars. Full vinyl roofs for hardtops come in black, white, blue, green, or brown.

Sportsroof models utilize a new three-quarter vinyl roof option that extends form the windshield rearward to a molding that connects to the rear edge of the bright drip molding.

MUCH SIMPLIFIED CONVERTIBLE TOP

The top linkage of the convertible is revised for 1971 so that the rear seat shoulder and elbow room is increased 11 inches from 1970. This extra room is gained by a wider stack and a simplified linkage

Rear seat and shoulder room is increased eleven inches this year in the convertible. Few people seemed to care, however, as Ford sold not much more than 6,000 units.

which fits lower into the well. One arm of the linkage is eliminated and another redesigned in the simplification which also gives the interior roof area near the rear seat a neater appearance. Ford also replaced the hinged, two-piece folding glass window with a tempered, semi-flexible one-piece window, and moved the top latches from the side rails to the top area above the windshield. In this position, the driver can release both latches without moving from his seat; and with the new rear window can lower the top without zipping out the rear window.

An optional protection package, new this year, included body side protective molding with color-keyed vinyl inserts and bright front lower valance guards with black rubber inserts. Another new option, front and rear twin, vertical bumper guards with black rubber inserts, was added this year and should not be confused with the valance guards of the protection package.

NEW LOOK AT THE REAR

The rear appearance is completely new but uses the standard Mustang theme. For the first time, the triple lens configuration of the taillamps contains the backup lights mounted in the center lens. The outer edges of the taillamps are rounded with a trapezoidal shape to blend with the contour of the sheet metal, and as always, the gas tank filler cap is centered in the panel between the taillamps.

STILL FANCIER INTERIORS

Interiors, although sporty, are more luxurious than ever, especially with the new optional power electric windows and rear window electric defroster. Standard high-back bucket seats are of a new thin shell design for 1971 with considerable comfort. A new "mini" console is standard for the first time in Mustangs and houses the gear selector lever and a slide-out ash tray at the back for rear seat passengers. The optional console, a virtual wall between front seat passengers, not only offers ample storage space, ash tray, and electric clock, but doubles as a center arm rest. Mach I and Grande consoles are accented by a simulated wood grain.

New color-keyed molded quarter trim panels utilize long (10.8"), integral arm rests with pull-type door handles. Upholstery includes six standard vinyl interior colors (five in convertible); six

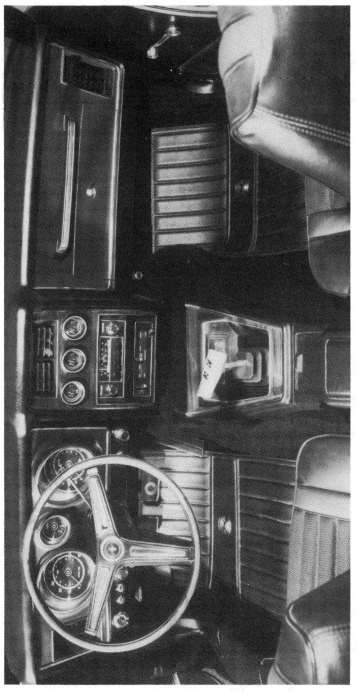

The sports luxury character of the 1971-73 Mustangs is revealed in the 1971 Mach I. The Hurst shifter is standard with a four-speed Ford transmission.

knitted vinyl colors in Mach I Sports Interior option and convertible; five cloth/vinyl trims in Grande; and two knitted vinyl and four cloth/vinyl trims in the Decor Group.

The Decor Group also added extra exterior features that included color-keyed outside dual racing mirrors with remote control for the left-hand mirror, bright and black rocker panel molding, wheel lip moldings, and wheel covers.

The Sports Interior option for the Mach I and sportsroof cars with V-8 engines includes knitted vinyl high-back bucket seats with accent stripes, the Instrumentation Group, door trim panels with integral pull handle and arm rests, color-accented deep-embossed carpet runner, deluxe instrument panel black applique with wood-tone center section, bright pedal pads, and a rear seat ash tray.

Although the rear seat and trunk are very small (as always), a new Sport Deck Rear Seat option joins the trunk and fold-down rear seat, allowing bulky or long items to be carried.

ALL-NEW PANEL FOR 1971

The completely-revamped dash for the 1971 models includes an instrument cluster with two large dials and one small dial grouped in front of the driver. The warning lights are fitted in the left dial; the smaller center dial is the fuel gauge; and the right dial is the speedometer/odometer with high-beam indicator.

The optional Instrumentation Group, however, put a tachometer in the large dial to the left plus oil pressure, water temperature, and alternator gauges in the center of the dash in a box or console. This console also contains the radio, heater, and air conditioning controls, plus two of the four air conditioning ducts (or extra storage box when A/C is not ordered).

The new "DirectAire" ventilation is a system in which floor level and/or instrument panel registers can be used to direct fresh air to the interior for windows-up, quiet ventilation, free of dirt and dust. Registers at each end of the instrument panel are adjustable and can be shut by moving the louvers to the extreme position. Knobs control the floor level outlets.

WIDER CAR, BETTER HANDLING

The greatly-improved riding and handling characteristics derive from the revised front suspension geometry of the wider stance and

The Boss 351 super car is an impressive-looking piece of machinery. Ford offered it for just the 1971 model year. 1971 gave the buyer his last chance to buy a Mustang factory super car.

the longer wheelbase. The wider stance reduces lean on turns, while the one-inch longer wheelbase naturally smooths the ride over rough surfaces. Mustangs with 351-4V and larger engines contain the staggered rear shock arrangement for increased traction, even if the buyer chose not to buy the competition suspension.

Competition suspension includes heavier duty springs, shocks, and front stabilizer bar, plus a rear stabilizer bar, and the staggered rear shocks on cars with the 351-4V and larger engines.

IMPORTANT STEERING CHANGES

Cars with the competition suspension have a variable ratio steering gear that is a new feature in 1971. The variable ratio system has a gear ratio of 16:1 at the center that varies to 13:1 at either extreme with overall ratios varying from 20.2:1 to 16.4:1. The advantage of this system is to provide more steering wheel movement on the straightaway, and somewhat less steering wheel movement in cornering or parking situations.

Cars with standard suspension use a new constant ratio system which uses an overall power steering ratio of 22.1:1 or a manual ratio of 27.7:1, each with a turning diameter of 39.8 feet. Of importance this year is the fact that the two new power steering gears use a new integral design with all components except the pump and connecting hoses mounted in the gear housing.

WIDER, LONGER AND LOWER

The wider front tract of the 1971's equals 61.5″ for a substantial 3.0″ increase over last year, while rear track increased 2.5″ to 61.0″. Bumper to bumper length increased 2.1″ to 189.5″, while the width of 74.1″ showed a 2.4″ increase. Height of the hardtop measures 50.8″; the convertible measures 50.5″; while the sportsroof measures the lowest at 50.1″. These correspond to about a half-inch lowering from 1970. Approximate weights of the base hardtop, sportsroof, and convertible equalled 3,087, 3,057, and 3,209 pounds respectively. Trunk capacity remained low, however, with 9.5 cubic feet in the hardtop, 8.3 cubic feet in the sportsroof, and a barely usable 8.1 cubic feet in the convertible. Fuel tank capacity dropped to 20 gallons on all models.

1972:
Start of the Last Roundup

As it was difficult six years earlier to distinguish a 1966 model from the 1965 Mustang, the 1972 models are equally difficult to tell from their 1971 counterparts. Of course, after a major restyling the previous year, neither model was ready for much more than refinement. Back in 1966, that refinement remained an absolute minimum because of record sales of over a half million, and lack of threatening competition in the sporty, specialty car field that Mustang completely dominated.

For 1972, increasingly stringent government emission control and safety requirements added since the Sixties brought unnecessary styling and engineering refinements to a near halt. In fact, for the first time in over 12 years Detroit automakers failed to introduce an all-new passenger car. Mustang and other ponycars continued to occupy a smaller part of the new car market.

SALES DOWN BUT STILL LEADING

Production for model year 1972 equalled 125,093 for Mustang, which compared well to 68,651 Camaros, 53,702 Cougars, 29,951 Firebirds, 27,176 Javelins, and 16,142 Barracudas. Mustang remained the best-selling car in its field while experiencing a 16% drop in sales. Its closest competitor, the Chevrolet Camaro, recorded a notable 40% slide in production from the 1971 model year. It looked

143

like ponycars were entering their last roundup. Meanwhile, the four-cylindered Chevrolet Vega and Ford Pinto racked up impressive sales of 394,592 and 347,822 respectively after a strike-hampered start in 1971. Many of the people that bought Mustangs and Camaros in the Sixties chose Pintos and Vegas in the early Seventies.

ENGINES ON REGULAR, SIX MODELS

The 1972 Mustangs differ from the 1971 offerings in several areas. For the first time, all engines run on regular fuel and the largest is the 351 cubic-incher. Horsepower ratings for these de-tuned and low compression engines are based on net horsepower, corresponding to the power remaining after the deduction of accessory equipment. Although the Boss 351 sportsroof was advertised for sale in early 1972 sales brochures, it was dropped before production. The model year lineup for 1972 is identical to 1971 with respect to body number:

Body	
#63D	Two-Door Fastback—Standard
#65D	Two-Door Hardtop—Standard
#65F	Two-Door Hardtop—Grande
#63R	Two-Door Fastback—Mach I
#76D	Convertible—Standard

The two-door hardtop, Model #65D, continued as the most popular Mustang in the stable; Ford built 57,350 of these with a base cost of $2,679. Standard equipment included the following: 250 CID-IV six; three-speed, floor-mounted and fully synchronized manual transmission; E78 × 14 belted bias-ply black sidewall tires; concealed windshield wipers; rocker panel and wheel lip moldings; lower back panel applique with bright molding; color-keyed dual racing mirrors; recessed exterior door handles; wheel covers; curved ventless sideglass; DirectAire Ventilation; heater/defroster; all-vinyl seat trim; high-back bucket seats; bonded door trim panels with pull-type handles and arm rests; mini-console; color-keyed carpeting; courtesy lights; deluxe two-spoke steering wheel with woodtone insert; lighter; reversible keys; keyless locking; steel guard rails; Uni-Lock Harness; Twice-A-Year Maintenance; and the Ford Motor Company Lifeguard Safety Features similar to last year.

The three basic body styles saw little change in 1972, but Ford dropped the Boss 351 trimmed sportsroof. Mustangs retained muscle-car "cosmetics" without the ultra-high performance.

LUXURY GRANDE, DISAPPEARING CONVERTIBLE

The Mustang Grande, Body Type # 65F, retailed for $2,865 with the standard features of the hardtop plus the following: Lambeth cloth and vinyl seat trim; black instrument panel appliques; electric clock; bright floor pedal trim; dual color-keyed racing mirrors with remote control LH mirror; dual bodyside paint stripe; vinyl roof covering, interior trim fabrics in five colors; wheel covers; rocker panel molding; wheel lip molding; and bright belt weatherstrip retainer. Production of the luxury-appointed Grande increased 609 units for 1972.

Ford offered the Mustang convertible for another year, but, with declining sales, its end was ever more clearly in sight to the analyst. Production increased almost 300 units for the soft top, Body #70D, indicating somewhat renewed interest. For the big Ford, 1972 was the last year of the convertible. The Mustang would be offered but one more year in this form. The base price of $2,965 included features listed for the hardtop plus the following: five-ply power-operated vinyl top with easy-fastening latches; color-keyed boot; tinted windshield; glass backlite; bright upper back panel molding; knitted vinyl seat trim; molded door panels with integral pull handles/arm rests; and black instrument panel appliques.

The sportsroof retailed for slightly more than the hardtop—$2,736. Of this model, Body #63D, 15,622 were produced in model year 1972, and its standard equipment added the tinted glass backlite and a fixed rear quarter window (unless optional power windows were ordered). The Mach I sportsroof, however, listed for $3,003 and outsold the standard sportsroof by 12,000 units, offering the basic features of the sportsroof plus the following: 302 CID V-8; E70 × 14 belted, bias-ply WSW Wide Ovals; competition suspension; choice of hood with or without NASA-type hood scoops (302 V-8 only); color-keyed front spoiler/bumper; color-keyed hood and fender molding; honeycomb texture black grille with integral sportlamps honeycomb back panel applique; black or argent painted lower body; front and rear valance panels; rear tape strip with Mach I decal; Mach I front fender decals; and wheel trim rings and hub caps.

JUST FOUR ENGINES & STRANGE HPs

The Mustang engine lineup underwent its greatest change in 1972 after a year of transition in 1971. One six-cylinder and four V-8's, counting the limited production 351-HO, make up the complete engine list. The 315 took honors as the largest volume engine; and, for the first time, all engines burned regular gasoline. The durable 429 Cobra Jet was dropped, just as it was ready for its second year of availability in all models. Prior to 1971, fitting the monstrous 429 required cutting and fabricating, a fact that lengthened the use of the older 428 block.

Horsepower ratings represent power supplied at the rear of the transmission with accessory equipment installed and operating; i.e., water pump, alternator, air conditioning, emission controls, power steering, etc. This industry-wide shift to net horsepower ratings made for some very unfamiliar figures.

The 250 CID six, continued again in 1972, yielded a net horsepower rating of 99 at 3,600 rpm with the single one-barrel Carter carburetor and 8.0:1 compression ratio. The three-speed manual transferred power to a 3.00 rear axle ratio that could be ordered with traction-lok. The optional Cruise-O-Matic use the higher speed 2.79's or optional 3.00's, each orderable with traction-lok. The four-speed manual was not offered with the six.

License plates reveal the year of this hardtop, or it would be difficult to tell it from a '71. Ford sold 18,045 of these Grandes in 1972.

The 302-2V, standard engine of the Mach I and optional for other body styles, rated 141 horsepower at 4,000 rpm with a single two-barrel Autolite carburetor and 8.5:1 compression ratio. The economy 302 used either the three-speed or optional Cruise-O-Matic as the four-speed was not listed in catalogs. Rear axle ratios listed are identical to those of the six-cylinder.

Ford built the 351-2V in Cleveland and Windsor form for use in all model Mustangs. It netted 164 horsepower at 4,000 rpm with the single two-barrel Autolite carburetor and 8.6:1 compression. The four-speed was not listed with this engine. The standard three-speed, however, uses a 2.75 rear axle ratio with a lower 3.25 optional, either with traciton-lok. The Cruise-O-Matic listed the same setup of standard and optional gear ratios.

PERFORMANCE 351 & HIGH PERFORMANCE VERSION

The 351-4V is the basic performance engine of the 1972 lineup, called the 351 CJ. Introduced late in the 1971 model year, this engine mounts the single four-barrel Autolite carburetor and rates a 248 net horsepower at 5,400 rpm with a low 8.0:1 compression ratio. The four-speed manual and the Cruise-O-Matic were both optional with the 351 Cobra Jet in another one of those situations where no transmission is standard. The four-speed (offered in the wide ratio only this year) came with a 3.50 rear axle or an optional 3.25, again each available with traction-lok. The automatic transmission reversed the ratios, 3.25 standard and 3.50 optional.

Ford also built a high-performance type engine called the 351-HO that is a modified version of last year's Boss 351. Changes include lowering the compression ratio to 8.8:1 to permit the burning of regular fuel and installation of a camshaft with a much higher valve lift for intake and exhaust. Camming is still mechanical; however, the net horsepower rating is 266 at 5,400 rpm with the single Autolite carburetor mounted on a high-rise aluminum manifold. Cars equipped with this engine, although minus the Boss name, have the standard features characteristic of the Boss 351, including a four-speed manual transmission, F60 × 15 RWL tires, dual exhausts, staggered rear shocks, competition suspension, a special cooling package, 3.91 traction-lok axle, electronic rpm limiter, 80-amp battery, collapsable spare tire, and power disc brakes.

VERY FEW OUTSIDE CHANGES

With respect to the exterior look of the 1972's, changes are nearly non-existent from last year.

Product planners revised the optional protection package and added a new decor group. The protection package of 1972 contains the bright bodyside molding with vinyl insert, plus bumper guards front and rear that are attached to the front of the bumper. These twin vertical guards with rubber insets give protection in low speed collisions such as would occur while parking.

The new decor group, for either the hardtop or convertible, consisted of a honeycomb black grille with integral sportlamps, color-keyed front spoiler/bumper, color-keyed hood and fender molding, black or argent lower bodyside paint with bright chrome molding, and wheel trim rings and hub caps. With this option the hardtop or the convertible took on the look of a Mach I. Also available with the decor group was the bodyside tape stripe in black or argent.

The Mach I sportsroof continued to offer the performance-oriented styling with its low-slung silhouette, optional NASA-type hood scoops, tape stripes, Mach I identification, urethane spoiler/bumper, etc. The looks of a real GT car are there, but the performance-developed engines are either gone (most notably the 429 Cobra Jets), or modified by increasingly stringent government emission controls (for example, the high output 351).

Other factory-installed option/accessories include a rear deck spoiler for the sportsroof and Mach I cars, front and rear bumper guards, tinted glass, door edge guards, and extra cost Ivy or Gold color glow paint.

INSIDE CHANGES & BUZZER REMINDERS

With respect to the interior look of the 1972's, Ford made several changes. A positive seat belt reminder system, outboard rear seat belt retractors (added after December 1, 1971), an optional AM/FM stereo radio with a new "mini" design, and an upgraded standard interior for convertibles separates the '72's from their 1971 counterparts.

When the ignition is "On," the transmission in gear (forward or reverse), and the front seat belts not pulled from their retractors the distance used to buckle up, a warning light and buzzer "remind" the

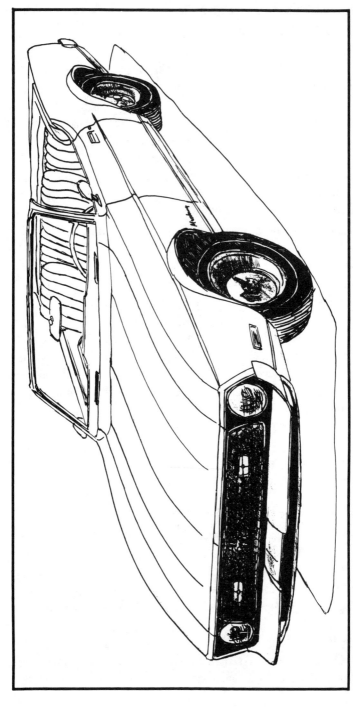

Either the hardtop or convertible could take on the look of a Mach I with the honeycomb black grille with integral sportlamps, color-keyed front spoiler/bumper, color-keyed hood and fender moldings, black or argent lower bodyside paint with bright chrome molding, and wheel trim rings and hub caps.

occupants to fasten their seat belts. Pressure on the front passenger's bucket seat activates a switch that reminds its user to buckle up, ever if that occupant happens to be a watermelon.

A common practice in 1972 was to pull the belts from their retractors enough to de-activate this system, and then tie the belt in a knot so it would not retract.

Rear seat belts, also added to the production line after December 1, 1971, came with retractors installed in a hidden position below the seat with the extending seat belt guide located between the seat and the side interior of the car.

The AM/FM stereo with its smaller "mini" size this year includes a built-in speaker in each front door and allows for five FM and five AM push-button stations.

CONVERTIBLE INTERIOR UPGRADED

The standard interior for convertibles, upgraded in 1972, includes a knitted vinyl seat trim, deluxe two-spoke steering wheel, a rear seat ash tray, deluxe molded door trim panels, and special instrument panel appliques. Other factory-installed option/ accessories include the convenience group, the Mach I sports interior option, door edge guards, intermittent windshield wipers, color-keyed vinyl front floor mats with carpet inserts, and adjustable five-way tilt steering wheel (with power steering required). The convenience group includes automatic seat back release, glove box lock, parking brake reminder light, headlamp reminder buzzer, courtesy lights under instrument panel (standard on convertibles), plus trunk, map, glove box, and underhood lights.

SUSPENSIONS AND DIMENSIONS STAY THE SAME

With respect to riding and handling characteristics, the 1972's parallel the 1971's. Competition suspension, staggered rear shocks, as well as the variable ratio steering returned. Standard suspension cars use the constant ratio steering system with an overall power steering gear of 22:1 and an overall manual steering gear of 30.2:1.

With respect to dimensions and capacities, the 1972's also parallel that of the 1971's. Wheelbase remains 109 inches; the bumper-to-bumper length of the car equals 189.5 inches, same as last year. Fuel tank capacity for 1972 equals 19.5 gallons, down a half gallon from 1971.

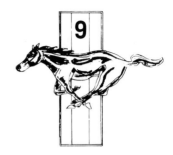

1973:

The Last of the First

For 1973, Mustang received a minor facelift plus enough refinements and improvements to set it apart from the 1972 cars. The most noticeable change is the new front grille look and the use of the blade-shaped urethane front bumper on all models. These bumpers withstand the five-mile-per-hour static impact as required industry-wide by the federal government.

The engine line-up remained the same as 1972 except for the dropping of the high output 351. Because federal standards required that each engine/axle combination be test run in duplicate for 50,000 miles, the number of rear axle ratios stabilized at about two per engine. Front suspension and brakes saw some minor improvements, while the increasingly popular radial tires were offered on the Mustang for the first time.

In the early seventies, automotive writers speculated that the Mustang nameplate might soon share bodies and running gear with Ford's intermediate-sized Torino due to the continued slide in the popularity of the ponycar and its steadily increasing size. But as it turned out, declining sales combined with the continuing requests for a smaller Mustang with the spirit of the first cars (1964, 1965, 1966.) This culminated in the introduction of a completely new "Mustang II" in 1974 on a 96-inch wheelbase.

LAST CONVERTIBLE IN 5-BODY LINEUP

The 1973 models, then, are interesting for several reasons. First, they represent the last of the "first generation" cars that evolved from that most famous Mustang introduced a distant nine years previous in the spring of 1964. Also, although the other Ford Division lines dropped convertible production at the end of the 1972 season, Mustang continued through 1973 with the soft top.

The last convertible Ford Division built was a 1973 Mustang. For one more year, the lineup consisted of the following:

Body # 63D   Two-Door Fastback—Standard
      #63R   Two-Door Fastback—Mach I
      #65D   Two-Door Hardtop—Standard
      #65F   Two-Door Hardtop—Grande
      #76D   Two-Door Convertible—Standard

The two-door hardtop, Body #65D, held its position as the most popular body style; about 38% of the total model year run of 134,867 consisted of the standard hardtop. Its basic equipment included the 250 CID six, fully-synchronized manual transmission with three-speed floor shift, new Energy-Absorbing Bumper System, color-keyed urethane front bumper, E78 × 14 belted bias-ply black sidewall tires, concealed windshield wipers, rocker panel and wheel lip moldings, lower back panel applique with bright molding, bright outside rectangular rearview mirror, recessed exterior door handles, curved ventless side glass, DirectAire Ventilation, heater/defroster, all-vinyl seat trim, mini-console, high-back bucket seats, color-keyed carpeting, courtesy dome light, deluxe two-spoke steering wheel with woodtone insert, lighter, reversible keys, "keyless" locking, Steel Guard Rails, Reminder System with Uni-Lock Shoulder/Lap Belts, plus all Ford Motor Company Lifeguard Design Safety Features.

GRANDE, SPORTSROOF, AND MACH I FEATURES

The Mustang Grande, also in its last season, accounted for about 19% of total production. Body #65F is the luxury version of the basic hardtop. For $2,946, or $186 more than the regular hardtop, the Grande included the following additional features: color-keyed duel racing mirrors; vinly roof with Grande script;

The 1973's use the new "cross hatch" grille with vertical inboard parking lights/turn signals and flanking headlights with bright headlight doors.

unique bodyside paint stripes; unique wheel covers; trunk floor mat; Lambeth cloth and vinyl seat trim; deluxe instrument panel with black camera case/woodtone appliques plus Grande plaque, and a panel-mounted electric clock.

The sportsroof, Body #63D, held a much smaller 8% of the total production in 1973. Retailing for $2,820, the sportsroof offered the standard features of the hardtop plus a fixed rear quarter window (except with optional power windows), and a tinted glass backlite.

Again, the Mach I trimmed sportsroof accounted for more sales. About 26% or 35,440 of the 1973 Mustangs produced were Mach I's. Designated Body #63R, it cost but $213 more than the standard-equipped sportsroof but offered the following extra equipment: a 302-2V V-8; competition suspension; choice of hood with or without NASA-styled hood scoops; E70 × 14 belted bias-ply Wide Ovals; color-keyed dual racing mirrors; color-keyed hood and fender moldings; honeycomb texture black grille with integral sportlamps; black rear panel applique; rear tape stripe with Mach I decal; wheel trim rings and hub caps; and bonded door trim panels with pull-type handles and arm rests.

DOUBLED SALES FOR LAST CONVERTIBLE

The two-door convertible, Body #76D, retailed in base form for $3,102, making it the most expensive Mustang of the lineup in base form. Sales of the soon-extinct Ford convertible nearly doubled for 1973, for obvious reasons. Exactly 11,853 of the stylish convertibles accounted for almost 9% of total 1973 model year sales, as buyers grabbed their last chance at a Ford convertible.

Standard equipment included those features listed for the hardtop plus a four-ply power-operated vinyl top in white or black with easy-fastening latches, a color-keyed boot, tinted windshield, glass backlite, bright upper back panel molding, knitted vinyl seat trim, deluxe molded door panel appliques, and power front disc brakes. Convertibles also have two courtesy lights—one on each side of the car under the instrument panel that take the place of an interior dome light.

ONE PERFORMANCE ENGINE REMAINS

The 1973 engine lineup, consists of the 250-IV six, plus the 302-2V, 351-2V, and 351-4V V-8's with a selection of transmissions

156

Hardtops built from 1971-73 have a design feature known as "tunnel backlite" in which the rear window is recessed between roof pillars that slope from the back of the roof to the rear deck.

and rear axle ratios similar to last year. In fact, specifications for the 99 horsepower six-cylinder read the same as last year with an identical combination of transmission and rear axle ratios. The same statement is true of the popular 302-2V, except that the Ford carburetor is called by the name of Motorcraft starting in 1973.

Changes begin with the 351-2V. For 1973, the three-speed manual transmission was not available with this engine. Instead the Cruise-O-Matic was a required option and the one transmission mated to the 351. The standard 2.75 rear axle ratio remained with the 3.25's optional, and either gear with traction-lok. The 351-2V is the one engine that could be ordered with ram air this year, in which case the 3.25's are standard rather than the higher speed 2.75's. With the single two-barrel Motorcraft carburetor and 8.6:1 compression ratio, the 351 yielded a representative 164 horsepower at 4,000 rpm. Power front disc brakes were another mandatory extra cost option with this engine.

One performance-type engine remained in the 1973 Mustang lineup, the 351 Cobra Jet. With single four-barrel Motorcraft carburetor and a low 8.0:1 compression ratio, the Cobra Jet rated a net 248 horsepower at 5,400 rpm. A descendant of the famous Boss engines of 1969, 1970, and 1971, the Cobra Jet's main performance features include four-bolt main bearing caps, a specially selected crankshaft of cast nodular iron, magnafluxed (x-rayed) connecting rods, mechanical camshaft, high load valve springs, and dual exhausts.

Power front disc brakes and competition suspension were required extra cost options with this engine. Either the four-speed manual (wide ratio) or the Cruise-O-Matic transmissions had to be ordered at extra cost also, as no transmission was standard. With the four-speed, the 3.50 rear axle ratio was standard and the 3.25 optional—either with traction-lok. With Cruise-O-Matic, the ratios were reversed, 3.25 standard and 3.50 optional.

URETHANE BUMPER ON ALL MODELS

Exterior styling continued with the "born of the track" look begun in 1971 and 1972. For 1973, however, Ford used the front urethane bumper on every model. Colored to blend with the body, it absorbs fixed carrier impacts up to five miles per hour. The bright

Sales of convertibles almost doubled in 1973, and for obvious reasons. This car was quite a bargain for just over $3,000.

159

metal rear bumper, however, with a less stringent federal safety standard, absorbs static impacts up to two and one-half miles per hour.

The new grille uses a "cross hatch" design made of plastic with a bright metal Mustang emblem in the center and new vertical parking lights/turn signals mounted at either end. The seven-inch single headlights flanking the grille are accented by bright rectangular headlamp doors on each of the models except for the Mach I and those cars with the optional Decor Group. The grille of the Mach I is described by Ford as a "black honeycomb" type with black rectangular headlamp doors.

The Decor Group, applicable to the hardtop or convertible, contains the Mach I-type "blackout" grille plus lower bodyside paint in black or argent with a bright metal molding at the upper edge, and hub caps with trim rings. The standard rocker panel moldings and wheel lip moldings are deleted on models equipped with the Decor Group.

Dual ram air induction, available only on cars with the 351-2V engine, features a NASA-type hood with two-tone paint and functional dual air scoops, hood lock pins, and "ram-air" engine decals. The air scoops, incorporating two vacuum-operated air control valves, permit forced air under high power, high rpm operation. A nonfunctional NASA-type hood was optional, however, without the ram air.

An Appearance Protection Group option this year included vinyl insert body side moldings, a spare tire lock, and door edge guards. With this option, Ford deleted the bodyside tape stripe of the Grande, and it was not available with the Mach I or cars with the Decor Group.

A deluxe bumper group in 1973 offered rear bumper guards with rubber inserts and a horizontal rub strip, while the standard twin rear bumper guards utilized the vertical rubber inserts.

FULL AND ¾ VINYL ROOFS IN SIX COLORS

The full-vinyl roof for the two-door hardtop came in six colors this year with a "C" pillar tri-color Mustang ornament. Those vinyl roof colors are white, blue, black, ginger (kiwi-textured), brown, and avocado. A three-quarter vinyl roof for the sportsroof and Mach

I models came in the same six colors, and the rear deck spoiler remained optional for the sportsroof and the Mach I. The 16 exterior color choices now included three metallic glow finishes at extra cost in gold, ivy, and the new blue glow paint. Ford also added forged aluminum wheels which replaced the optional-styled steel wheels of years past.

CONTINUED LUXURY INTERIORS

The "dual cockpit" interior styling also showed little change from the 1971 and 1972 cars. Standard features like the thin shell, high-back bucket seats, deluxe two-spoke steering wheel, and mini-console give each model a luxury-appointed interior before the added options and accessories. Factory-installed option/accessories include front color-keyed floor mats, AM radio (required with stereo-sonic tape system), AM/FM stereo radio (required with stereo-sonic tape system), AM/FM stereo radio (not available with the stereosonic tape system), stereosonic tape system with two front-door mounted speakers (requires AM radio at extra cost), SelectAire air conditioning (not available with the 250 CID six-cylinder engine in combination with three-speed manual transmission), console that included an electric clock, the convenience group, an electric rear window defroster (except on the convertible or cars with the six-cylinder engine), tinted glass complete, deluxe seat belts (standard on the convertible), sport deck rear seat, sports interior option, deluxe three-spoke rim blow steering wheel, tilt steering wheel (requires power steering at extra cost), leather-wrapped deluxe two-spoked steering wheel, interval windshield wipers, tinted windshield (as a limited production option for fleet sales, although standard on the convertible).

HANDLING ADAPTED TO RADIALS

Suspension changed slightly in 1973, tuned to accept both the new radials or the standard belted bias-ply tires. Ford engineers softened the ride with added suspension travel and reduced overall spring rates with longer, recalibrated shock absorbers. Softened rear suspension bushings also helped reduce ride harshness. The GR78 × 14 steel-belted radial tires gave an even smoother luxury car-type ride with an advertised tire life of 40,000 miles for the average driver.

The competition suspension, however, (standard on the Mach I), continued in 1973 with the front stabilizer bar, high-rate springs, and competition shock absorbers. All cars with the 351-4V, however, include a larger front stabilizer bar and staggered rear shock absorbers.

Ford added power front disc brakes as standard equipment for both convertibles and models powered by 351 CID engines. As another improvement, Ford increased the rear brake lining area on drum brake systems by eleven percent.

Dimensionally, the 1973's are the longest, lowest Mustangs ever built. Due to the new energy-absorbing bumper system, overall length of the Mustang increased a whopping 4.5 inches. Wheelbase remained at 109 inches, but the front tread width decreased a half inch to 61.0, and rear tread width equals 60.8 inches. Height of the hardtop, convertible, and sportsroof equals 50.7", 50.4", and 50.0", respectively.

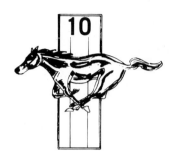

1964-1973:
Mustang Value Guide

The Mustangs produced during the model years 1964-1973 comprise what is generally know as the "first generation" cars, and a major group of special interest American automobiles. Although every car is collectible and desired by certain individuals with varying tastes in motor cars, specific body styles and models are, of course, favored by knowledgeable car buffs. Certainly, the 1964-65-66 models which have made such a hit with Americans will remain favorites. But, each model year contains cars that for one reason or another attract high interest. Convertibles of every model year are certainly highly prized as are GT's, Mach I's, and cars with high performance engines, to name a few. A guide to the value of each of the regular production Mustangs, therefore, is given. Approximate values of the GT-350's and GT-500's built by Carroll Shelby are also included, although their worth (in particular the early competition prepared cars) is highly speculative because of their rarity.

    The purpose of the following value guide is to give one an idea of the values of Mustangs according to model, body style, engine, and other special interest features. Condition, as outlined in the Vehicle Classes section, is of the most importance in determining value. Any car in "Excellent" or "Number 1" condition is worth a considerable amount of money; sometimes less for its special interest and more for its usefulness and clean looks. Very few cars fall into this category without considerable time and money spent in restoration. However, some original low mileage cars warrant this classification, although they are exceedingly rare, especially those cars with high performance capabilities.

Cars in "Number 2" condition are also very rare in original condition, especially the older models. Most Mustangs driving the streets rate a "Number 3 or 4" classification.

Many others remain in an undriveable state, about a "Number 5" classification, awaiting a total restoration of body, chassis, and interior. Some cars that will not even rate this "restorable" condition bring more money for the value of their parts than for a car in better condition, especially if they contain valuable options like Rally-Pacs, air conditioning, tilt steering wheels, high performance engines, traction-lok rear axles, hub caps, etc.

OTHER FACTORS AFFECT PRICE

Other factors not reflected in the guide affect value beside condition and the specific model. Prices vary in different parts of the country for the same automobile. Color is a factor not taken into account that sometime alters a selling price. A red convertible, for example, generally excites more interest than a green one. An anxious seller usually means a price below normal, while an anxious buyer can inflate the price.

Auction prices are very deceptive to the chance owner of a special interest auto like the Mustang. One with a passing interest in the old car hobby is likely to ask $4,000 for his car because he "heard of one going for that at an auction in Dallas," when actually his car is in poor condition and of a different body style/engine combination.

For these reasons, the following guide gives "ballpark figures" based on condition and model (as specific as necessary). Although values may not be exact, each Mustang is graded relative to the rest of the breed, and using the famous *Old Cars* class and value scheme, the most accurate and respected in the hobby of old car collecting.

VEHICLE CLASSES*

1) EXCELLENT: Restored to current professional standards of quality in every area; or original with all components operating and appearing as new.

*Derived by *Old Cars Newspaper*, 700 E. State St., Iola, Wisconsin 54945; and used in their *Old Cars Price Guide.*

2) FINE: Well-restored; or combination of superior restoration and excellent original; or extremely well-maintained original showing very minimal wear.

3) VERY GOOD: Completely operable original; or older restoration showing wear; or amateur restoration; all presentable and serviceable inside and out. Also combination of well-donw restoration and good operable components; or partially-restored car with all parts to complete and/or valuable NOS parts.

4) GOOD: A driveable vehicle needing no or only minor work to be functiona; or a deteriorated restoration; or a very poor amateur restoration. All components may need restoration to be EXCELLENT, but are mostly usable "as is."

5) RESTORABLE: Needs complete restoration of body, chassis, interior. Not driveable, but is not weathered, wrecked, or stripped to the point of being useful only for parts salvage.

Vehicle Classes

1964		5	4	3	2	1
Body #65A	2d hardtop	500	900	1400	2100	2800
#76A	convertible	600	1100	1700	2900	3500

Add 10% for cars with V8 engines.
Add 20% for cars with the 271 horsepower, 289 high performance engine.

1965		5	4	3	2	1
Body #63A	2d fastback, standard	550	950	1500	2200	3000
#63B	2d fastback, luxury	550	950	1600	2300	3100
#65A	2d hardtop, standard	500	900	1400	2000	2700
#65B	2d hardtop, luxury	525	925	1450	2100	2900
#65C	2d hardtop, bench seat	500	900	1400	2000	2700
#76A	convertible, standard	600	1100	1700	2900	3500
#76B	convertible, luxury	600	1200	2000	3000	4000
#76C	convertible, bench seat	600	1100	1700	2900	3500

Add 10% for cars with V8 engines.
Add 20% for cars with the 271 horsepower, 289 high performance engine.
Add 25% for cars with the GT Equipment Group option.

		5	4	3	2	1
Shelby GT-350 -	2d fastback	1200	2000	3000	5000	7500
	2d fastback (R)	1500	2500	4000	7000	9500

1966		5	4	3	2	1
Body #63A	2d fastback, standard	550	950	1500	2100	2900
#63B	2d fastback, luxury	550	950	1600	2200	3000
#65A	2d hardtop, standard	500	900	1400	1900	2600
#65B	2d hardtop, luxury	525	925	1450	2000	2800
#65C	2d hardtop, bench seat	500	900	1400	1900	2600
#76A	convertible, standard	600	1100	1700	2800	3400
#76B	convertible, luxury	600	1150	1800	2950	3750
#76C	convertible, bench seat	600	1100	1700	2800	3400

Vehicle Classes

		5	4	3	2	1

Add 10% for cars with V8 engines.
Add 20% for cars with the 271 horsepower, 289 high performance engine.
Add 25% for cars with the GT Equipment Group.

Shelby GT-350 - 2d fastback	1000	1700	2500	4000	6500
Shelby GT-350 - 2d fastback (R)	1400	2200	3500	6000	8000
2d fastback (350-H)	900	1600	2200	3500	6000

1967

Body	#63A	2d fastback, standard	400	750	1250	1800	2500
	#63B	2d fastback, luxury	400	800	1350	1900	2700
	#65A	2d hardtop, standard	300	600	1000	1500	2100
	#65B	2d hardtop, luxury	300	650	1100	1600	2200
	#65C	2d hardtop, bench seat	300	600	1000	1500	2100
	#76A	convertible, standard	500	900	1500	2400	2900
	#76B	convertible, luxury	500	950	1600	2500	3100
	#76C	convertible, bench seat	500	900	1500	2400	2900

Add 10% for cars with V8 engines.
Add 20% for cars with the 271 horsepower, 289 high performance engine.
Add 20% for cars with the 390-4V Thunderbird Special.
Add 10% for competition handling package.
Add 25% for cars with the GT Equipment Group.

Shelby GT-350 - 2d fastback	700	1400	2000	3200	4500
2d fastback	800	1500	2200	3800	5000

1968

Body	#63A	2d fastback, standard	400	750	1250	1800	2500
	#63B	2d fastback, luxury	400	800	1350	1900	2700
	#63C	2d fastback, bench seat	400	750	1250	1800	2500
	#63D	2d fastback, deluxe bench seat	500	850	1500	2100	2900
	#65A	2d hardtop, standard	300	600	1000	1500	2100
	#65B	2d hardtop, luxury	300	650	1100	1600	2200
	#65C	2d hardtop, bench seats	300	600	1000	1500	2100
	#65D	2d hardtop, deluxe bench seat	300	650	1150	1700	2300
	#76A	convertible, standard	500	900	1500	2400	2900
	#76B	convertible, luxury	500	950	1600	2500	3100

Add 10% for cars with V8 engines.
Add 20% for cars with the 390-4V "Thunderbird Special".
Add 25% for cars with the 427-4V.
Add 25% for cars with the 428 Cobra Jet.
Add 25% for cars with the GT Equipment Group.
Add 40% for cars with the "California Special" trim.

Shelby GT-350 - 2d fastback	700	1200	1800	3000	4200
convertible	700	1250	2000	3100	4400
GT-500 - fastback	800	1500	2200	3800	5000
fastback (KR)	900	1700	2500	4200	5500
convertible	800	1600	2300	4000	5200
convertible (KR)	850	1650	2400	4100	5300

1969

Body	#63A	2d fastback, standard	350	650	1100	1600	2200
	#63B	2d fastback, deluxe	350	700	1200	1750	2400
	#63C	2d fastback, Mach I	500	900	1500	2200	3200
		(Boss 302)	800	1500	2500	3500	5500
		(Boss 429)	1000	1800	3000	4000	6000
	#65A	2d hardtop, standard	250	500	900	1400	2000
	#65B	2d hardtop, deluxe	250	550	1000	1500	2100
	#65C	2d hardtop, bench seats	250	500	900	1400	2000
	#65D	2d hardtop, deluxe bench seat	250	550	1100	1600	2200
	#65E	2d hardtop, Grande	350	600	1200	1700	2400
	#76A	convertible, standard	500	1000	1600	2500	3100
	#76B	convertible, deluxe	500	1100	1700	2600	3200

Vehicle Classes

1968 (continued)		5	4	3	2	1

Add 10% for cars with V8 engines (except for Mach I, Boss 302, Boss 429).
Add 25% for cars with the 428-4V Cobra Jet.
Add 30% for cars with the 428-4V Super Cobra Jet.

		5	4	3	2	1
Shelby GT-350 -	2d fastback	800	1300	2000	3100	4300
	convertible	850	1400	2200	3300	4000
GT-500 -	fastback	900	1500	2300	3500	5000
	convertible	950	1600	2400	3600	5200

1970

Body		5	4	3	2	1
#63A	2d fastback, standard	300	600	1000	1500	2100
#63B	2d fastback, deluxe	300	650	1100	1650	2300
#63C	2d fastback, Mach I	500	900	1500	2100	3100
	(Boss 302)	800	1500	2400	3400	5200
	(Boss 429)	1000	1800	3000	4000	6000
#65A	2d hardtop, standard	250	500	850	1300	1900
#65B	2d hardtop, deluxe	250	500	900	1400	2000
#65E	2d hardtop, Grande	350	600	1100	1600	2300
#76A	convertible, standard	500	1000	1600	2500	3100
#76B	convertible, deluxe	500	1100	1700	2600	3200

Add 10% for cars with V8 engines (except for Mach I, Boss 302, Boss 429).
Add 25% for cars with the 428-4V Cobra Jet.
Add 30% for cars with the 428-4V Super Cobra Jet.

		5	4	3	2	1
Shelby GT-350 -	2d fastback	800	1300	2000	3100	4300
	convertible	850	1400	2200	3300	4600
GT-500 -	fastback	900	1500	2300	3500	5000
	convertible	950	1600	2400	3600	5200

1971

Body		5	4	3	2	1
#63D	2d fastback, standard	300	600	900	1400	1800
#63R	2d fastback, Mach I	400	750	1250	1800	2400
	(Boss 351)	700	1300	2000	3200	4000
#65D	2d hardtop, standard	300	500	800	1300	1700
#65F	2d hardtop, Grande	325	650	950	1500	2000
#76D	convertible, standard	550	1200	1800	2800	3300

Add 10% for cars with V8 engines (except Mach I, Boss 351).
Add 30% for cars with the 429-4V Cobra Jet.
Add 35% for cars with the 429-4V Super Cobra Jet.

1972

Body		5	4	3	2	1
#63D	2d fastback, standard	300	600	900	1400	1800
#63R	2d fastback, Mach I	400	750	1250	1800	2400
#65D	2d hardtop, standard	300	500	800	1300	1700
#65F	2d hardtop, Grande	325	650	950	1500	2000
#76D	convertible, standard	550	1200	1800	2800	3300

Add 10% for cars with V8 engines (except Mach I).
Add 20% for cars with the 351-4V HO.
Add 20% for cars with the Decor Group.

1973

Body		5	4	3	2	1
#63D	2d fastback, standard	350	650	1000	1500	2000
#63R	2d fastback, Mach I	400	750	1250	1800	2400
#65D	2d hardtop, standard	300	500	800	1300	1700
#65F	2d hardtop, Grande	325	650	950	1500	2000
#76D	convertible, standard	600	1300	2000	3000	3600

Add 10% for cars with V8 engines (except Mach I).
Add 20% for cars with the 351-4V Cobra Jet.

All Mustang Engines

Six-Cylinders	Code*	Model Years
170-1V	U	1964
200-1V	T	1965-1970
250-1V	L	1969-1973
Small V-8's		
260-2V	F	1964/65
289-2V	C	1964-1968
289-4V	A	1964-1967
289-4V, H.P.	K	1965-1967
302-4V	J	1968
302-4V (Boss)	G	1969-1970
302-2V	F	1969-1973
Intermediate V-8's		
**351-2V	H	1969-1973
***351-4V	M	1969-1971
351-4V (Boss)	G	1971
351-4V (H.O.)	R	1972
351-4V (C.J.)	Q	1971-1973
Large V-8's		
390-4V	S	1967-1969
390-2V	Y	1968
427-4V	W	1968
428-4V (C.J.)	Q	1968-1970
428-4V (CJ-R)	R	1969-1970
429-4V (Boss)	Z	1969-1970
429-4V (C.J.)	C	1971
429-4V (SCJ)	J	1971

* The letter designating the engine code is the last letter appearing in the vehicle identification number (or warranty number) located on the vehicle identification plate. This plate (or decal) is attached to the inside rear edge of the driver's side door.

** Cleveland or Windsor (Windsor only, 1969)

*** Cleveland

All Mustang Transmissions

Transmission	Code*	Years
Three-Speed Manual	1	1965-73
Four-Speed Manual	5	1965-73
Four-Speed Manual (Close Ratio)	6, E	1969-71, 1972-73
Three-Speed Automatic (C4)	6	1965-66
Three-Speed Automatic (C4) (Select Shift)	W	1967-73
FMX Automatic	X	1969-73
Three-Speed Automatic (C6) (Select Shift)	U	1967-73

NOTE: C4—Applies to: Six cylinders

V-8's prior to 1967

Small V-8's '67-'73 (except h.p. V-8's)

FMS—Applies to: Intermediate V-8's (except h.p. 351's)

C6—Applies to: Large V-8's

H.P. V-8's

---

* Transmission codes appear on the vehicle identification plate as well as on a small plate on the side of the transmission.

All Mustang Rear Axles

Axle	1965	1966	1967	1968	1969	1970	1971	1972	1973
2.35					F				
2.50				0					
2.75			8(H)	1(A)	2(K)	2(K)	2(K)	2(K)	2(K)
2.79				2(B)	3	3	3	3	3
2.80	6(F)	6(F)	6(F)	3(C)	4(M)	4(M)	4(M)	4(M)	
2.83	2(B)	2(B)	2(B)	4(D)	5	5			
3.00	1(A)	1(A)	1(A)	5(E)	6(O)	6	6	6	.6(O)
3.07						B	B		
3.08					C(U)	C			
3.10					7				
3.20	3(C)	3(C)	3(C)	6(F)		8			
3.25	4(D)	4(D)	4(D)	7(G)	9(R)	9(R)		9(R)	
3.50	5(E)	5(E)	5(E)	8(H)	A(S)	A(S)	9(R)	A(S)	9(R)
3.89	8(H)	8(H)					A(S)		A(S)
3.91					(V)	(V)		(V)	
4.11	9(I)	9(I)	9(I)				(V)		
4.30					(W)	(W)	(Y)		

NOTE: Letters or numbers in parentheses denote locking axles.

* Rear axle ratio codes appear on the vehicle identification plate as well as on a tag bolted to the differential case.

Index

B

Blocks, 427 & 428	82
Boss 302 & Boss 429	98, 114
Boss 351	130
Brake improvements	71
Buzzer reminders	149

C

California Special	88
Challenger V-8	34
Chassis mounts	70
Cleveland engine	118
Cobra jets	120
Convertible	155
Convertible & fastback	96
Convertible interiors	151
Convertible sales	156
Cougar	61

D

Decor, paint & protection options	85
Demand for mustangs	49
Dimensions	68
Dimensions & capacities	42
Dimension of 1970's & last Shelbys	124
Disc brakes	42
Desirability, Distinctions, & accents	38
Drag Pack	120

E

Engines	77, 116, 144, 146

F

Fancier interiors	138

Flair group of options new	123
Ford's performance image	13
Former extras now standard	79
Four speeds & cruise-o-matic	36
Four-speed with two ratios	116
427 & 428 blocks	82
428 Cobra jet	104
429 Cobra jet	134
Full & ¾ vinyl roofs	160

G

Grande & convertible features	113
Grande, Convertible & sportsroof features	129
Grande, Sportsroof & Mach 1	155

H

Handling adapted to radials	161
Handling	140
HD & competition suspension packs	75
Heavy-duty units helped suspension	40
Hertz 350-H	58
Holman & Moody	134
Hurst	114, 123

I

Iacocca, Lee	14
Interiors	88, 106, 122, 161
Interior options	68
Interior variations	39

L

Length & weight	104
Luxury grande	145

M

Mach 1   95
Maverick   93, 111
Minor changes distinguish
  model years   54
Model T & A   11
Model year in detail   20
Model years, minor changes
  distinguish   54
Motors, Mustangs powered by four
  different   52
Mustang I   15
Mustang II Serious prototype   17
Mustang GT-350, GT-500   42, 58
Mustangs powered by four
  different motors   52
Mustang value guide   163
Mustang was a cougar   17

N

New body styles   63
1962 Mustang 1 effective teaser   15
1964, 1964 ½, 1965 same model   31
1967 Mustang   61
1967 styling changes   66
1968 models   77
1969 Mustang   93
1970 Mustang   111
1973 Mustang   153
Number of Mustangs built   49

O

Options   32, 40, 67
Options/accessories   24
Options, decor, paint & protection   85
Options, flair group new   123
Option list   51

P

Panel   140
Performance   25
Performance engines   156
Performance image, Ford's   13
Performance 351   148
Power years   22
Production & body line-up   127
Project T-5   14
Public reaction   29

R

Rally-Pak   40, 52, 66
Rear styling & spoilers   105
Road racing & drags   98

S

Sales   143
Select shift   66
Sheet metal changes   105
Shelbys   89
Shelby & the GT-350   42
Shelby GT-500   75
Shelby Mustang 1966-1970   25
Simplified convertible top   136
66 options   56
Standard features   95
Standard hardtop   113
Standard panel   57
Standard six   34
Steering changes   142
Styling   24
Styling changes   84, 120
Super car   130
Suspension   57, 89, 107
Suspension & dimensions   151
Suspension, heavy-duty units
  helped   40
Suspension improvements   124
Suspension packs, HD &
  competition   75

T

Ten engines   98
The Debut   27
Thunderbird Special V-8   82
Turino/Torino   14, 153
302-V-8   82
352 Windsor   102
390 block   64
390 block, virtues   64
260 V-8   34
289 V-8s   36

U

Urethane bumper   158

V

V-8's   52, 132
Variations of new panel   68
Vehicle classes   164
Virtues of the 390 block   64

W

Wedge   84
Wildest boss   102
Windsor & cleveland 351S   118
Windsor engine   102